POSTSCRIPT

POSTSCRIPT

*A collective account of the lives
of Jews in West Germany
since the Second World War*

Edited and translated by

KAREN GERSHON

LONDON
VICTOR GOLLANCZ LTD
1969

PRINTED IN GREAT BRITAIN
BY EBENEZER BAYLIS AND SON, LTD.
THE TRINITY PRESS, WORCESTER, AND LONDON

To the Memory of
Victor Gollancz

7

Dear Livia,

When I returned to my home town, Bielefeld in Westphalia, in 1963, after an absence of twenty-five years, I was surprised to find that there were still Jews living there. I had left Germany at the age of fifteen in the winter of 1938 with a children's transport to come to England; during the war my parents died in concentration camps. After the war, I did not want to be informed about anything concerning Germany, which I had once loved with all my heart; I returned, completely ignorant about the postwar period, merely to revisit the places where I had been a child.

At the beginning of the century, nearly a thousand Jews lived in Bielefeld; now there are fewer than sixty. It used to be, and it is today, fairly typical of the German communities. When I met some of the Jews there I wanted to find out what it felt like to live as a Jew in Germany today, and during the next five years this gradually led me to the exploration which has resulted in this book.

Yours sincerely,
Karen Gershon.

Jerusalem, November 1968.

CONTENTS

Most of the material for this book was collected during the winter 1967/68 which I spent in Israel at the invitation of President Shazar. I am grateful to him, and also to the late Dr. Shaul Esh, who guided my early reading. I am grateful to the many people—mainly students—who allowed me to interview them, and to all those who responded with diaries, old letters, recollections and comments to my appeal for information which appeared in Jewish newspapers all over the world.

I collected some of the material in the Wiener Library, London, the Central Zionist Archives of the Jewish Agency, Jerusalem and the Yad Vashem Archives, Jerusalem; I owe thanks to the librarians there who helped me and also to those of the Jewish National and University Library, the Hebrew University, Jerusalem, where I did most of my reading.

For general information I relied upon Dr. Harry Maór's *Ueber den Wiederaufbau der jüdischen Gemeinden in Deutschland seit 1945* (1961) and Dr. Walter W. Jacob Oppenheimer's *Jüdische Jugend in Deutschland* (1967); I also read through twenty years of the *Allgemeine Wochenzeitung der Juden in Deutschland*. Below is the list of other published material from which I have quoted; I am, naturally, very grateful to all those concerned who have given me permission to quote their words.

The stanza by Nelly Sachs appears in the translation of Christopher Holme.

I owe thanks to my family, especially to my husband, for tolerating my long absences from home so that I could produce this book.

In English
Books: Zorach Warhaftig, Uprooted (1946); The Jewish Travel Guide (1953); Leo Schwarz, The Redeemers (1953); European Jewry Ten Years After (1956); C. I. Krapalik, Reclaiming the Nazi Loot (1962); Norbert Muhlen, The Survivors (1962); David Wdowinski, And we are not saved (1963); Dr. Hendrick van Dam, The Jewish Community in Germany (1966); Amos Elon, Journey through a Haunted Land (1967); American

Jewish Year Books (1946–1947). Periodicals, Newspapers, etc.: Commentary, David Bernstein, Europe's Jews (1947); Norbert Muhlen, In the Backwash of the Great Crime (1952); Hal Lehrman, The New Germany and Her Remaining Jews (1953); Gershom Scholem, Jews and Germans (1966); A. J. R. Information (1946); Consultative Conference of Jewish Organisations (1955); The Toronto Telegram, Gordon Donaldson (1959); The World Union of Progressive Judaism (1965); The New Society, Neal Ascherson (1966); The Jerusalem Post, Moshe Kohn (1967).

In German

Books: Dr. Lothar Rothchild, Der Stein als Zeuge (1946); Dr. Benjamin Sagalowitz, Judentum und Deutsche (1949); Dr. Knud C. Knudsen, Welt ohne Hass (1950); Deutschland und das Judentum (1951); Prof. D. D. Paul Tillich, Die Judenfrage (1953); Erich Lueth, Deutschland und die Juden nach 1945 (1957); Wolfgang Jäger, Ed., Unsere jüdischen Mitbürger (1958); Heinz Ganther, Ed., Die Juden in Deutschland (1958/59); Peter Schönbach, Reaktionen auf die Antisemitische Welle (1960); Henry Görschler, Horst Reinhardt, Die Schande von Köln und Bonn (1960); Alfred Kantorowicz, Deutsches Tagebuch (1960); Joseph Melzer, Deutsch-Jüdisches Schicksal (1961); Heinz Liepmann, Ein deutscher Jude denkt über Deutschland nach (1961); Willy Brandt, Deutschland, Israel und die Juden (1961); Dr. Hendrick C. van Dam, Juden in Deutschland (1961); Karl Marx, Brücken Schlagen (1962); Dr. Salzberger, Christlicher Antisemitismus (1962); Vera Elyashiv, Deutschland—Kein Wintermärchen (1964); Carl Busch, Ed. Israel und Wir (1955–1965); Hans Rauschning, 1945—Ein Jahr in Dichtung und Bericht (1965); Eva Zipora Prijs, Die Einstellung der Münchener jüdischen Jugend zu Israel (1965); Franz Böhm, Walter Dirks, Ed. Judentum (1965); Leonard Freed, Deutsche Juden Heute (1965); Friedrich Oppler, Das Falsche Tabu (1966). Books on the Communities: Dr. Hans Lamm, Von Juden in München (1958); Ernst Simons-Köln, Geschichte der jüdischen Gemeinde im Bonner Raum (1959); Dr. Zvi Asaria, Die Juden in

Köln (1959); Hans Chanoch Meyer, Aus der Geschichte der Juden in Westfalen (1962); Ludwig Hellriegel, Geschichte der Bensheimer Juden (1963); Stefan Schwarz, Die Juden in Bayern (1963); Berent Schweinkörper, Franz Laubeuger, Geschichte und Schicksal der Freiburger Juden (1963); Theobald Nebel, Geschichte der jüdischen Gemeinde in Talheim (1963); Leben und Schicksal, Hannover (1963); Maria Zelzer, Weg und Schicksal der Stuttgarter Juden (1964); Jüdisches Schicksal in Paderborn (1964); Eugen Mayer, Die Frankfurter Juden (1966). Festschriften: Prof. Dr. Ernst Röth, Zur Einweihung der Synagoge in Stuttgart (1952); Die Neue Synagoge in Düsseldorf, (1958); H. G. Sellenthin, Jüdisches Gemeindehaus Berlin (1959); Zum 60. Geburtstag von Carl Katz (1959); Prof. Dr. Ernst Röth, Zur Wiedereinweihung der alten Synagoge zu Worms (1961). Periodicals, Newspapers, etc.: Jüdische Rundschau (1946); Mitteilungsblatt, Tel Aviv (1945–1950); Der Weg, Berlin (1946–1953); Jüdische Jugend (1956); Der Monat, Klaus Harprecht (1959); Mitteilingsblätter für die jüdischen Gemeinden in Westfalen (1959/60); Der Monat, Friedrich Torberg (1961); Germania Judaica, Köln (1960/61); Nachrichten für den jüdischen Bürger in Fürth (1958–1961); Der Spiegel (1963); Germania Judaica, Juden in Deutschland Heute (1963); Kontakte, Allgemeine jüdische Jugendzeitschrift (1962/63); Wir, Jugendgruppe der Synagogengemeinde Köln (1962/63); Blätter des Bielefelder Jugend-Kulturringes (1963); Jüdische Sozialarbeit (1960–1964); Münchener jüdische Nachrichten (1951–1966); Aufbau, New York (1945–1966).

EDITORIAL NOTE

I hope that the combination of the different voices will have the same effect as a conversation. Three groups of people have contributed to this book: Jews who are living in postwar Germany or who were living there when their contribution was uttered; whenever the contributor changes I have marked the beginning of the paragraph thus —. Comments by others are printed in italics, those provided by Jews not belonging to the first group (mainly contemporaries abroad) are marked ✡; those provided by non-Jews (almost always Germans) are marked †.

Most of the material I have translated from the German.

It seemed pedantic to insist upon saying 'West Germany' every time the country was mentioned; in fact most of the contributors do not do so. There are between 2–3 thousand Jews in East Germany; I am very sorry that not enough information about them is available to include them in this book.

POSTSCRIPT

. . . in spite of everything I still believe that people are really good at heart.

Anne Frank

I

THE SURVIVORS

✡ *Burdened with three sad infirmities:*
   with poverty, bodily ills, and Jewishness. (Heinrich Heine)
✡ *Writes the poet, that poverty and illness might be alleviated.*
But from the third: the Jewishness, nothing can save us.

— Those of us who are still alive have survived accidentally; we have not in any way earned our survival.

— I walked along slowly; I am not yet able to grasp what it means, no, I still cannot quite believe it; I am alive, I really am alive and the wide sky is above me. Dear God, why did you preserve me of all people—why should I have been chosen to be one of the survivors? I searched for my friends, but found only solitude; they did not even leave me anything to remember them by. Where was I to go—who cared what became of me—where should I look for my family? Everything gone—only I survived, and that was no consolation. I don't know where I went; I only felt that I had to run, to escape from myself, from my thoughts; I felt very miserable indeed.

— The 'happy survivors' are today the saddest, most tragic beings in human shape, morally, physically, spiritually, and psychologically ill, without home, house, family. Nobody can imagine what these survivors went through—with their own eyes they saw their closest relations led into the gas chambers: father, mother, wife, children, friends—and as they stood helplessly by they had only one wish: at once into the gas chamber with all the others, that would be best.

There is no prisoner who has not asked himself more than once: is this worth my survival? If I had only followed my family into the gas chamber, I would have been spared all this.

We were liberated.

Many knew that there were no relations waiting for them at home. They left the camp and went in another direction.

But many, and this is perfectly understandable, made straight for their homes, to look for their relations. Husband, wife, child, father, mother, brother, sister—where are you all? The former prisoner goes on searching; rarely does he find anyone.

It is pleasant to shut the eyes and to remember the past; with open eyes one encounters the astonished, questioning looks of the present. Are you still alive, Jew?

Once we had children, husband, wife, father, mother—it is impossible to continue living in this country, this town, this house, amongst the overwhelming memories of the past.

Such is our mental condition, physically we are completely exhausted; before we have had the chance to eat a square meal we are told of fresh casualties of antisemitism, even of pogroms here and there.

For these people, the war is not yet over. When will it be over? Will it ever be over? The heart will continue to bleed; body and soul will need a long time to recover.

Where are the doctors who could cure us quickly? Cure nerves, heart, lung, stomach and venereal diseases, without medicines and without provisions? Nowhere.

What are we to do? Make a new beginning here, start building a new life in this country? The answer in the depth of our hearts is clearly no. What is the use of staying here—away, the sooner the better.

Carrying a knapsack containing all we own, we set out—men and women, everybody is young, in the whole wide world there is only one destination: Eretz Israel.

We set off without knowing where we are going, with the thought that somehow we will manage to get there; we have had enough practice during the past few years in doing without, in fighting to survive.

We will have to get to a country in which we may be able to forget and to recover, but until then, who will help us 'happy survivors'?

— It would need a great many words to relate what we have

been through—we have been running a race with death. The five years were a martyrdom for us, especially the last three months. But we hope fervently that our energies will return once we are living again under conditions fit for human beings. We are still capable of working, although at the moment we are completely exhausted. Help us, help us! Do not keep us waiting overlong. We would like a chance to feel ourselves human . . .

✡ *I have seen thousands of Jewish survivors from the concentration camps, and spoken to many of them. The older generation, the people above fifty, have suffered most. They are physically and mentally ruined. One imagines that they will never be able really to recover. All the others—and they are the great majority—have survived their awful experiences astonishingly well. Naturally, most of them still show traces of hunger, of having been close to death for a long time, of the pain and torment of all that they have been through. The youngsters who have for years existed on a diet lacking in proteins and vitamins have obviously been arrested in their physical development—but their vitality, their hardiness, their zest for life is amazing. They are making a visible recovery . . . They have become capable and tough—no Jews have ever been as capable and as tough as these youngsters. They are not afraid: nothing worse than the concentration camps can happen to them; as far as they are concerned, there are no insuperable obstacles. Nevertheless, one thing is clear: their past experiences will always be with them. The concentration camps have left traces which can never be outgrown. This 'life' made no allowances for sensitivity, for honesty, for manners and morals, which are taken for granted by the rest of us. The law of the jungle was applied by the victims as well. What counted were brute strength and unquestioning egoism, and these often made the difference between living and dying. Hunger and fear create their own laws. People permanently under sentence of death— men and women, old or young—do not have the same moral code as people in ordinary life.*

— I had a very simple slogan: first survive, the rest will somehow arrange itself. And this helped me more than a thousand philosophical subtleties: it made me struggle and win through. The war ended and I had survived . . . A few days later I got

used to it . . . I began to wish for more: to be no longer lonely,
to know whether any of my relations abroad had survived.
Coming from Poland I knew: there were none of my family on
the continent any more.

† *The streets are crowded with the inmates of the concentration
camps. Those who foresaw a trail of violence spreading across the
country have been proved wrong, as far as I am able to judge from
here. I have the impression that the people are rather gay with the
relief of their own resurrection. This morning, six Jews who had been
liberated from Belsen came into the farmyard. The youngest of them
was eleven years old. He was fascinated and enthralled by a picture
book, as if he had never seen one before. Our cat drew from him the
same reaction of amazement, as if it were a dream phantom.*

† *They are drifting about the streets in their thousands. Their
clothing is makeshift and insufficient, they have a miserable few
belongings, and they are everywhere. They are at a loss; they don't
know where to go or what to do.*

— Are we supposed to go back where we came from? Who is
waiting for us? There is nothing for us at home, there is no 'at
home' any more. All we owned has been taken, those we loved
have been killed. Somebody ought to tell us what we should do.

✡ *Only a few were able to celebrate a happy reunion with
family and relations, and on those occasions they usually learned of
the death of other members of the family and of friends. And there are
many who did not know of any survivors at all.*

✡ *Everywhere hundreds of thousands of men and women and
children, all of whom have lost the natural bonds of family and who
are today solitary individuals. All the children are orphans—most
of the middle-aged people have lost their children. Members of large
families have become the sole bearers of their name.*

✡ *The overwhelming majority of the Nazi camp survivors are
single survivors of exterminated families.*

✡ *. . . the tragedy of the Jews, who have become a people of
orphans and bereaved parents.*

✡ *The state of health is much better than expected. Generally
speaking, those who survived were strong and young people.*

✡ *As a result of the Nazi extermination policy, the majority of the*

Jewish survivors consists of young people. Men outnumber women, and there are very few children or old people among them.

✡   *When liberated from the concentration camps, the Jews were sociologically abnormal. All the older people and all the children had been exterminated. The intellectuals, the professional people, the leadership, the sick, the weak, had perished. Chiefly those survived whose labour or skill was useful to their captors.*

—   One of the saddest aspects of the Jewish catastrophe in Europe is the almost complete extermination of the Jewish intelligentsia. Of all our poets, writers, artists, musicians, scientists and scholars, very few have survived.

—   Consider that almost none of the spiritual leaders have survived, because they were least suited to carry sacks of cement . . .

✡   *There are neither rabbis nor Jewish scholars amongst the survivors.*

✡   *Only one rabbi survives in all of Germany.*

✡   *It is strange indeed and almost incomprehensible that the surviving Jews have not taken any revenge or shown any signs of hatred. Doubtless, they are behaving according to Jewish tradition, which teaches quite plainly that the purpose of human existence is love and that he who hates lives in vain.*

—   We have no desire to revenge ourselves, rather, we are inclined to feel ashamed because of what has happened.

—   God, my God and God of my parents, I am grateful to you and grateful to my parents that I have not been brought up to hate my fellow men. Immediately after the liberation, when I was put in charge of a small village, I had to protect the German population against the fury of the displaced Russians and Poles. I was glad to see that my comrades distributed chocolate to the German children and were nice to them, although during the four years of their imprisonment they had preached hatred and planned how to take their revenge. There was no case of murder or any violence on the part of Jewish survivors.

—   There was no bloodshed. We did not take revenge. We did not rob people or loot places. The hatred we felt was too deep, the contempt too great. There was only one way for us to express our reaction: we wanted to get out of Germany.

— When American troops entered Cologne on 6th March 1945, between thirty and forty Jews came out of their hiding places.

Most of the survivors met in front of the former synagogue; in the days after the liberation this was the general meeting place of any surviving Jews. An attempt was made to clear at least one of the rooms of debris. Then they went to the Jewish hostel and began to work there, clearing rubble, replacing doors and windows. Before long, it was possible to hold the first divine service. Soon afterwards the survivors held their first meeting. By this time the number had increased to fifty. A sign in German and English was hung on the door of the community centre. People started arriving, wearing the thin, striped concentration camp uniform; they came from every direction, exhausted and in need. Some had got lifts in military vehicles, others had made their way to Cologne on foot. The first appeals for help from Theresienstadt reached Cologne towards the end of May. Dr. Adenauer, who was then the mayor, had already made the necessary arrangements for sending transportation to Theresienstadt. Of the four to five thousand Jews there at the time of the liberation only about five per cent remained. Eighty people, men and women, were in the first group to return to Cologne. A second group of between sixty and seventy people arrived in August. In the meantime, a number of survivors had returned from other concentration camps, so that there were altogether about three hundred Jews in the town.

— Hanover was occupied by American troops on 10th April 1945. At that time, about twenty to thirty members of the original Jewish community remained in the town; if one includes those who were not Jewish by religion but were persecuted as Jews because of their race, there may have been altogether about one hundred people. After a few days an emergency committee was formed, which was provided with an office in the town-hall. The function of this committee was to render first aid to survivors returning from the camps and to provide them with money and additional ration-cards. One of the first and most urgent duties was to arrange for the burial of twenty-three Jewish corpses, concentration camp victims, which were in the sanatorium for consumptives. Not even coffins were available. The bodies were wrapped only in sheets. Apart from this we cared for the survivors returning from the camps. Many of them were in need of hospitalisation. Besides medical attention and food they also needed comfort and advice. With the help of the municipality we ourselves were able to organise the return of the survivors from Theresienstadt. We were provided with a lorry and with food for the journey. The town also put at our disposal a house, to provide the survivors with accommodation.

— In spite of the destruction of Hamburg and the attending hardships, a new life began for us at once. Already on the day of the liberation our little office was besieged by people who had been living illegally and were in need of immediate help. A few hours after the Gestapo had fled from it, we managed to install ourselves again in the community centre, which had not been damaged at all. With the help of the relief organisations we arranged for the return from Theresienstadt of the remaining Jewish survivors who belonged to Hamburg and northwest Germany, and provided a temporary hostel where the older people could be accommodated. The Nazis and the war had between them destroyed all the synagogues, but we managed to make the synagogue belonging to the former old people's home fit for use.

✡ *The first Jewish relief organisation to make its appearance in Germany was the 'Joint',* which opened offices in Berlin, Frankfurt, Munich, and many other towns. For the German Jews and even more for the Jewish Displaced Persons it became the centre of their hopes, the beginning of their return to life.*

— I returned to Dortmund from Theresienstadt towards the end of July 1945 and found three other Jews who had returned. We tried at once to collect all the survivors together. Some we met in the streets; the others we went in search of. After a great deal of trouble I managed to arrange our first meeting in the only restaurant remaining in the centre of the town (the town centre had been completely destroyed). But only a very few people

*American Joint Distribution Committee Inc. (1914). Organises and administers welfare, medical and rehabilitation programmes and services and distributes funds for relief and reconstruction on behalf of needy Jews overseas.

showed up and so we decided to make another attempt. This second meeting already drew the attendance of between fifteen and twenty people. A provisional committee was elected and I was delegated to take up our case with the municipality. I succeeded before long to make contact with the authorities, especially with the housing department, though at that time the civil government was hardly functioning. At about this time the town provided a bus to fetch the remaining survivors from the Theresienstadt concentration camp. At the end of July the bus returned with the surviving members of the former community. As no houses or flats were available, most of them were accommodated in a hostel. In the meantime, those who had been persecuted for religious or racial reasons had elected a committee from amongst the former concentration camp inmates. The municipality opened a department to help the Jewish survivors. All those concerned were meant to report to it; they were registered for the allocation of accommodation and of clothing coupons. It has to be remembered that everything was rationed and that not even things that were urgently needed could be got without coupons or rationcards. Survivors received a small extra allocation. We all drew public assistance.

— Some fifty Jews came together in Frankfurt, former residents who had been released from the concentration camps and other survivors who found themselves there accidentally. Amongst the ruins of the half-destroyed town and all the totally destroyed Jewish places, the survivors began or rather, attempted to begin to resuscitate the Jewish community. Provisionally divine services were held in the only Jewish house to remain relatively undamaged, and gradually its rooms were transformed into a simple but dignified synagogue.

— After the survivors had returned from Theresienstadt, divine services began to be held in the Jewish hostel. Prayers were usually led by refugees who were passing through, Jews from Eastern Europe who had some knowledge of Jewish tradition. In this way, the few remaining German Jews became familiar with East European customs and pronunciation.

— In Stuttgart, the Jewish citizens who gathered together were very few. They were not homogeneous but formed three distinct groups: those who had remained Jews by religion, those who had before or during the years of persecution abandoned the Jewish religion and those who had adopted the Christian faith but were Jews by race.

— There are 8,000 Jewish survivors in Berlin. Of these, 4,700 owe their lives to the fact that they were partners of mixed marriages, i.e. they were married to Christians. 1,900 have returned from the concentration camps, most of them from Theresienstadt. 1,400 are the survivors of a group of 5,000 who were living illegally during the persecution.

— Those who returned to Berlin from forced labour and concentration camps found not a town but a gigantic expanse of ruins . . . The Jewish survivors were exposed to the same hardships, the same desperate situation, as all the other citizens of the town. The innocent had to suffer with the guilty . . . Many of the survivors who returned were seriously ill, many who survived did not return because they were too ill to leave the camps; some of the survivors died on the way home. Almost all of those who returned from the concentration camps continued to bear the physical consequences of their experiences for the rest of their lives.

— Hardly one of us still possessed a house or a flat, or had any other possessions. During the years of the persecution, everything we had owned had been gradually taken away from us; we had been expelled from our homes, their contents had been sold, and our businesses had been liquidated.

✡ *Because of the confiscations (of their belongings as well as of their clothing coupons) and in consequence of their deportation, the Jews have nothing at all. Clothing and blankets are completely unobtainable.*

✡ *Everything normally considered essential in daily life, provisions and clothing, accommodation and medical supplies, was almost entirely lacking. There was also a tremendous personal, human need, for a word of advice, for encouragement, for contact with the rest of the world, and therefore a need for trained and willing people who could understand the problems and offer advice and guidance.*

— All our endeavours of the first few hours, days, weeks, were dictated by the need to relieve the appalling lack of accommodation, provisions and clothing amongst the survivors who were starving, exhausted and destitute. The first communal activity was a continuous struggle to ease the hardships and to turn the theoretical liberation into practical fact.

— The mayor of the town at once put some money at our disposal. This enabled us to give financial assistance to all those who returned completely destitute from the concentration camps. Through the good offices of the military authorities we were also given the use of a hotel, which provided accommodation for the first groups of survivors, who had been wandering about from place to place with nowhere to go. The kitchen of the hotel was equipped to provide our people with three hot meals daily. Since then, the Jewish population has continued to grow and our work has increased.

— We have to be prepared to expect an average of 600 people daily, who will have to be dealt with and sent on. We have to be ready to accommodate these people for one or two days only. But we have no proper housing for them and no beds. Just imagine what it means when new arrivals have to sleep on the floor. Many of the survivors wear pieces of military uniform, or they are still wearing camp clothing.

The Polish-Jewish committee has provided us with a table for medical examinations.

On demand, we provide the survivors from the concentration camps with medical treatment and with medicines; the Jewish hospital will take anybody we send them.

We shall organise a bath for every concentration camp survivor and refugee.

We have to be prepared to expect a total of between 50,000 and 60,000 survivors and refugees in transit. Up till now our committee has cared for 10,000 Jews. We feed them, house them, and provide them with something for the journey.

We have given assistance to all Jewish travellers regardless of what country they have come from.

— The first important task of the new community was to help

between six and seven thousand refugees from the districts east
of the Oder. At that time every refugee received the fabulous
sum of 35 *Reichsmark*. Furthermore, food and clothing had to
be made available especially to those who were returning from
the concentration camps. We had also to carry on negotiations
with the military authorities in order to achieve some consideration for the special position of Jewish citizens and equal treatment for them in all the four sectors.

They are bitterly disappointed because they had expected the
liberation to make a much bigger difference to their lives. What
they mind most is the indifference towards them of the British
and American authorities. The Jewish survivors feel that little
has changed in Berlin since the coming of the Russians, except
that the food shortages have become worse. They remain a
suffering minority; nobody cares what becomes of them and they
will soon have reached the limits of human endurance.

. . . so that if help does not arrive quickly, the problem posed
by the Jewish survivors in Berlin will largely be solved by their
suicide and death.

The negotiations with the liberators were extraordinarily
difficult. To begin with, they treated the German Jews as if they
were Germans.

The situation is altogether very complicated. There are four
different zones, there are the different parties, there are the
different groups of refugees. There is the question of the transportation and the distribution of provisions and other supplies.
Amongst the thousands of problems which beset their administration, the occupying authorities are tempted to simplify things
by overlooking the 'small' problems of the few surviving Jews.

THE CAMPS AFTER LIBERATION

— The situation among the victims is not improving; there are still 200 dead every day. Have I been chosen by providence to bury the rest of the survivors? The doctor told me today that there is no point in vaccinating people because everyone is bound to get typhus. Strange, for four years I looked forward to the day of liberation and now I am prepared to look forward to death. I am not afraid; death would be a way out of this hell. The first of May—what daydreams my comrades and I had about it before we were liberated!

✡ *13,000 Jews died in Bergen-Belsen camp between the middle of April and 12th June 1945. Their names are unknown because the Germans burned the lists. Even now, three months after liberation, there are twenty funerals every day, and Jews by the tens of thousands are in hospitals.*

✡ *Most of the Jews from Eastern Europe were not removed from the camps, where they continued to be short of food and did not receive the necessary medical attention. German Jews who were released from the camps were handed over for care to the German civil authorities, on the grounds that these Jews were German nationals. Conditions began to improve late in June, when the 'Joint' was granted permission to extend relief.*

Jewish relief work of primary importance has been done by the Jewish chaplains and soldiers in the US and British Armies, and by the Palestine Jewish Brigade. They were the first to enter the liberated areas. They organised relief activities before any international or voluntary relief agencies could arrive. They were the spokesmen for the displaced persons before the military authorities. They also helped the DP's to communicate with relatives abroad. But above all they—particularly the soldiers of the Jewish Brigade—helped to bolster the morale of the DP's.

✡ *I have visited the former concentration camp Buchenwald. The spirit of these people becomes even more striking as I think about it. Some—many—are physically and psychologically ruined, perhaps for life. But others are eager to begin to live again, an inspiration to those of us who never had to love life as much as they did in order to survive.*

After leaving the camp, I realised that I had learned little about the experiences of these Jews. They had been too busy talking about the future.

How much vitality, optimism and lust for life animated these people, whose experiences should have destroyed their faith in mankind.

— The most important thing to be said two months after our liberation is that conditions for us have changed hardly at all. Almost everywhere, our people remain imprisoned behind barbed wire; in many camps there is still not enough to eat and everywhere there is a great shortage of clothing. The average state of health has improved—those who were very weak have died.

Unfortunately, mentally we are even worse off. What hurts most is that of all the many Jewish organisations which exist in every country one can think of, so far not a single one has managed to visit us or to prepare the way for some sort of relief measures. As far as we are concerned, things are becoming more urgent. A general repatriation has already begun. There are Jews from several countries who do not want to return to where they came from. Now what?

✡ *There is no feeling of newly found freedom. People are not allowed to walk outside the camp. It is not true that there is a quarantine—former camp SS officials are living in the neighbouring town.*

✡ *At Turkheim, 450 Jews continue to live in the double barbed wire enclosure which still retains the deadly electrical apparatus. At Buchberg, 1,000 Jews are living in a former powder factory. Built in barrack style, the camp is dilapidated and very much overcrowded. Such items as soap, toothbrushes, linen, laundry facilities etc. are unobtainable. Plumbing, where it exists, is inadequate for the numbers it has to serve.*

✡   *In Landsberg camp there was overcrowding and underfeeding,
lack of adequate clothing, and housing so bad that it had been
rejected as unfit for German prisoners of war. Some 6,200 Jews were
living in quarters meant for 4,200. The Jews resent having to accept
American food and clothing as an act of charity; they would prefer
to receive German food and clothing as a portion of their claim on
Germany.*

✡   *Allach is a badly equipped miserable-looking concentration
camp a few miles from Dachau. There are nearly 3,000 Jews there,
the major groups being Poles, Hungarians and Rumanians. About
one quarter of the population are women. Their condition appears to
be much better than that of the men. This I found generally to be the
case.*

✡   *Three months after their liberation, men are still walking about
the streets in the ragged, striped prison trousers doled out to them by
the Nazis in the concentration camps. They have nothing else to
change into. Little things like cigarettes, sweets, toothpaste, are as
rare as gold. An attempt has been made in a few of the camps to
enliven the monotony of camp life by holding dances in the open air
and by showing films. But these are exceptions. The inmates have no
money with which to buy a little distraction in a neighbouring town.
Many are quite willing to work; many young people would like to
join the American Army. Some have laid out little gardens, others
busy themselves as carpenters—but the responsible officials in the
allied military government do nothing whatever to help them. The
division of Germany into four zones of occupation has complicated
the problem.*

✡   *No provision has been made for the most urgent requirements;
people are expected to sleep in pairs on wooden planks . . . All the
arrangements are totally unsuitable for this group of people, eighty
per cent of which are old and frail. If this is where they are expected
to spend the winter, most of the old people will not survive.*

*These 600 Jews have been living in a concentration camp under
the most awful conditions; they had hoped that after the war they
would find ways and means to rejoin their children, their brothers
and sisters. Now they are again kept in a camp, guarded as if they
were criminals.*

The conditions under which they are obliged to live could not be worse; not only is the food insufficient, they are insufficiently cared for in every respect. We had assumed that the transit camp would be a place in which the old people would be able to recover from all they have suffered during the past few years.

The people here are kept isolated from the world outside.

✡ *Four months after their liberation thousands of these poor people are still prevented from returning home because there is no transport for them, because they are too ill to be moved, or for other reasons. And at home nobody is waiting for them—no wife, no child, no father, no mother, no brother and no sister. By their hundreds of thousands these are lying in the mass graves and millions of them have been incinerated in the crematoria of the extermination camps.*

✡ *The greatest worry of all the inmates of these camps is the fate of their families. Most of their relations have been killed, and they have lost contact with those who managed to escape. The lack of information worries them and makes them feel depressed. Everyone is most anxious to know whether any member of his family is still alive . . .*

✡ *The wireless broadcasts information, search advertisements are published, particulars are circulated to the offices, the Central Committee, the Jewish Agency; the files and the survivor-books are consulted—every single case is important, is sacred, is urgent. The Search-Department receives thousands of letters from all over the world and sends out just as many. The Jewish World Congress possesses in London the largest index of names and particulars of half a million Jews who have survived. Thousands of them have been put in touch with their families.*

✡ *The Search-Service conducted enquiries concerning the Jewish families who had been dispersed across the whole continent. In most cases 'positive' information meant bad news, confirming the death of one of the deported.*

✡ *The situation is still in constant flux as a result of the general chaos caused by the continuous arrival of Jewish DP's. There is an internal movement from one occupation zone to another and from camp to camp in search of emigration possibilities or better living conditions; the military authorities frequently move the Jewish DP's*

2

either from one camp to another or from the cities to the camps; there is also a constant infiltration from neighbouring countries. No provision is made for listing the Jews as a special group regardless of their formal nationality.

✡ *It is the policy of the military government in occupied territories to place all refugees on an equal footing regardless of their religion or nationality. This results in the situation that Hungarian, Austrian or German Jews, who were only recently liberated from concentration camps, are officially regarded as 'enemy aliens' and treated as such. They are expected to return to the towns and villages where they had 'come from', that is, from where they had been taken to concentration camps.*

✡ *There is an increasing trend among Jewish refugees and displaced persons to renounce their nationality. This is true not only of German and Austrian Jews, but also of Jews from Poland, Hungary, Rumania and Czechoslovakia. The great majority of the Jewish DP's in the U.S. zone in fact refuse to be registered according to their nationality. They have been registered either as 'stateless' or among the 'unclassified'.*

✡ *Life in the concentration camps also had its positive side. There, the individual was even weaker and more defenceless than elsewhere. He was in need of support. And so necessity forged small communities, especially amongst young people, capable of withstanding every test ... These small, inseparable groups who practise an often superhuman comradeship can be found everywhere.*

✡ *In many cases, the Jews complain about the overcrowding of the camps, but resist when the authorities arrange a transfer of a surplus of people from one camp to another. They are longing for communal ties, they are accustomed to their surroundings, and the word 'transfer' terrifies them.*

✡ *The Jews present the American military administration with a special problem. They are generally unwilling to return to their country of origin, their reactions always seem excessively emotional, they keep themselves apart from the other citizens of their respective countries, and they continue to cross the borders illegally in large numbers. The Americans feel compelled to devise a special treatment for the sake of this relatively small group of people. This causes resentment at the higher levels. At the middle and lower levels and especially in the executive branches, people are unwilling to recognise the need for a special way of dealing with the Jewish problem.*

† *As matters now stand, we appear to be treating the Jews as the Nazis treated them, except that we do not exterminate them. (Earl G. Harrison, U.S. Representative on the Intergovernmental Committee on Refugees)*

✡ *Striking evidence of Nazi technique were barbed wire fences, armed guards and the prohibition against leaving camp except by special pass. With few exceptions, no efforts have been made to rehabilitate the internees. And while Jews are still living in insanitary and crowded conditions, under guard and without the opportunity of communicating with the outside world, the Germans continue to live normal lives in their own homes. Many displaced persons, after long periods of near starvation, are still receiving a diet of principally bread and coffee.*

— The daily ration—too much for people to starve and not enough to keep them alive.

✡ *The principal problem is an insufficient supply of food. The people who live in these camps were for years kept on a starvation diet in concentration camps and are now hungry and undernourished. Much bitterness is caused by the fact that they have been put on the same ration-level as the civilian population, which still has food reserves. It means that their suffering during the last years has not been taken into consideration and that they are treated no better than our former enemies. Furthermore, there is a lack of clothing in every camp. Many people still wear their prison uniform.*

✡ *Until 19th November no important distribution of clothing had taken place, and this in spite of the cold. No underwear, no overcoats, very few blankets and shoes have been distributed so far. This is one of the causes of the great danger of new epidemics.*

Not one briquette of coal, not one piece of wood was distributed in the camp up to 19th November. It is evidently too late now to provide adequate heating for the winter, and this is the main factor in the spreading of epidemics.

The administration of the camp does not permit any discussion of emigration plans among the displaced persons. This does not exactly help the morale of the inmates, and they need strength of mind to meet the hardships of the winter.

If conditions remain as they are, and all the efforts of the voluntary agencies cannot help much, the result will be that by the spring no more than 25,000 of the remnant of European Jewry will survive. There is no doubt that the army could manage the necessary supplies, transportation and services to meet the emergency within a few weeks, at the eleventh hour and three weeks before Christmas.

It is openly admitted and officially announced that we will not be able to avoid some trouble from the Germans because of the general winter situation. We can be sure that the Jews in and outside the camps will once more be the first victims.

— Suffering continues to be our badge.

✡   *Liberated but not free—that is the paradoxical situation of the Jews. In the concentration camps they had the overwhelming hope of being saved. This was what kept them alive, what helped them to bear their sufferings and to survive. Now they have been saved . . . they have been given no new source of hope.*

— In the meantime, the promising future has become the grim present.

✡   *The DP-camps are destroying the extraordinary ability of these people to recover at least psychologically—much as the concentration camps destroyed their bodies.*

✡   *Many of the survivors made use of the opportunity provided by the repatriation transports to return to their countries of origin in order to search for missing relatives; but others endeavoured, with the help of the Jewish Brigade and of Jewish soldiers in the Allied armies, to reach the coast in the hope that from there they would be able to continue their journey to Eretz Israel. After a short time those who had gone east began to return: instead of their relatives the refugees had found only the ruins of their former communities, and so they came back to the DP-camps, and with them came thousands of Jews who had survived the war by hiding in the forests, or with the help of false 'Aryan' papers. By the end of the summer of 1945, there were again 40,000 Jewish refugees in Germany. They were in need of first aid and medical treatment, food and clothing. They were concerned above all in securing recognition as a special national group and fought for the establishment of separate camps for Jews. Already in July 1945, delegates from the camps in and near Munich met and elected a common committee. They issued the statement that there was only one solution: Eretz Israel, for their problem and the problem of the Jewish people as a whole.*

✡ *Some of the people who were amongst the first to return to Poland, Hungary or Rumania are now coming back because they found it impossible to stay there. The reasons they usually give are the antisemitism of the local population and their own psychological reaction to being in places which have become Jewish graveyards. They went back to look for their relatives and when they found out that they were the only surviving members of their families, they tried to escape their feeling of loneliness by fleeing their town and their country.*

✡ *A few of them have made the experiment of returning to Poland. After a very short time they showed up again in the camps of Germany with terrible news: in Poland nothing has changed. Not only are Jews received with cold hostility—from the moment they return their lives are continually in danger. Hundreds of Jews have been killed in Poland since their 'liberation'. The tiny remnant of Jews left there clamours impatiently to leave the country. The news brought by refugees from other countries in Eastern Europe is not much better. Really, the situation is paradoxical: Jews from the east are fleeing into Germany.*

✡ *There is a fixed pattern to the wanderings of these Jews. They return to their country; they look round and do not find any of their families, relatives and friends; they bid farewell to the ruins of their homes and their communities; then they turn west, towards the strategic passageways, to the 'gates' that lead to Palestine and to other lands overseas.*

— We have been rescued but we have not yet been saved.

III

THE HOMELESS

✡ *The new DP-camps were established on the sites of the former extermination camps, in the vicinity of the crematoria and the mass graves (Bergen-Belsen, Landsberg, Feldafing, Foehrenwald, etc.). Schools, hospitals, nursery schools and agricultural training centres were organised, and on the parade grounds from which the condemned had once marched to their execution, Hebrew melodies predicted the regeneration of the Jewish people.*

— Near the old camp, which had to be burned down, a new camp was established in the barracks which had formerly been used by the guards. This provided refuge not only for the former prisoners but also for the many homeless people who were arriving from other countries. The name Belsen acquired a new and special meaning.

The camp became the centre of Jewish cultural life. The main concern was the practical preparation for life in Israel. With the help of the large Jewish relief organisations, various training courses were established; altogether the help of these organisations was of overwhelming importance in the everyday life of the DP's in Belsen.

Out of nothing grew schools which provided an excellent standard of education, children's homes, workshops, a printing press, a newspaper, and last not least Sammy Feder's concentration camp theatre. From the beginning, the former prisoners, both men and women, helped to care for the sick and played their part in establishing the camp.

The survivors were possessed by a terrific urge to be doing things.

— The formation of local and central committees and the existence of the camps created centres of Jewish life. The DP-camp Bergen-Belsen in the midst of the Lueneburger Heath grew into a small Jewish town with its own mayor, some kind of justices of the peace, and it even had its own police force. But above all it became a place of constant discussion and cultural activity.

✡ *It is a grave mistake to treat them as sick people who need to be cured. They have enough moral stamina and strength to rehabilitate themselves, given some slight help from outside.*

✡ *These men and women with the Buchenwald and Sachsenhausen and Auschwitz tattoo on their arms have an indescribable vitality, a deep air of purpose. They have given mental and moral rehabilitation priority over the material. They organise schools before they build dining-halls; they call for books before they ask for clothing.*

✡ *I had steeled myself to see the living skeletons and broken human beings such as were liberated by the Allied armies eight months ago. I met upright men and women who were, to all outer appearances at least, normal, strong and healthy. In a miraculously short time their will to live has transformed them from pieces of broken humanity into a new type of Jew. It is a new type altogether —not a better, not a worse type, but a different type. They are not apathetic, but full of fighting spirit, distrustful of the world, relying on no one but themselves; they do not beg, they reject charity—they demand their rights. They speak a new Yiddish, a language which is dynamic and sharp—they have their poetry, their songs, their theatre and their press, but they do not seem to write with a pen— they write as if with a hammer.*

— The human debris shaped itself into people, and the people recognised social obligations. Committees, schools, administrations, newspapers were created. The society began to be organised.

✡ *These people who have suffered years of humiliation were possessed by an urge for cultural regeneration and mental activity. Their self-consciousness, frequently manifested in a downright ostentatious manner, soon found expression in the Jewish press, newly created for this very purpose.*

— The Jews who have been liberated in the camps want to 'catch up'. Catch up—intellectually. They were starving for a word of Judaism. And so everything is set in motion, hurriedly,

to satisfy this intellectual hunger. Wherever there are a few Jews
—in a hospital, in a barrack, in a camp—they produce newspapers and magazines. Newspapers of from 12 to 24 and more
pages, magazines often of up to 80 pages. They issue thousands,
tens of thousands of copies.

Advertisements are missing, but there is a constant column:
We are looking for relatives . . .

These newspapers are appearing in almost every language, but
mainly in Yiddish and Hebrew.

✡ *Nursery schools, schools and courses were organised, so that no
Jewish child remained without an education. Sports clubs, amateur
threatrical companies and orchestras have been established. The
streets in the camps have been named after cities and settlements in
Palestine.*

✡ *Jewish life has been rapidly and efficiently organised on both a
local and central basis. Jewish committees, democratically elected,
have taken over responsibility for all internal problems within the
camps. A central committee of liberated Jews has been finally
recognised by the military government.*

✡ *The Federation—Sheerith Hapletah—had as its principal
purpose the protection of the survivors in the American zone of
occupation and representation of the people vis-à-vis the military
and civilian authorities, including Jewish relief and political agencies
in Palestine and the United States. (The phrase Sheerith Hapletah
is biblical in origin, being used in the book of Chronicles to describe
the remnant that survived the Assyrian conquest. Amongst the
liberated Jews it was used to denote the surviving remnant of the
destruction during the Second World War, but as time went on, it
came to be used with ideas and shades of meaning that are only partly
suggested in the Saving Remnant.) To the leaders, the Sheerith
Hapletah was no less than a revolutionary spearhead in the movement for national redemption.*

— We ourselves and we alone are responsible for the shaping of
our future. We have to begin again right at the beginning and it is
necessary for us to forget the benefits to which we may feel ourselves entitled because of all that we have been through. We can
and we shall fight against the grossest injustices suffered by our

people; but in the meantime we have to act responsibly for the sake of our future. Up to a certain point we will have to forget the past. I know, it is almost impossible, but if we cannot manage to do this it will only be to our own disadvantage and we will face even greater difficulties.

— Nine months after our liberation we are still suffocating in the camps. We are to become the subject of a study, committees are to decide what is to be done with us. We are stateless, homeless. International politics is choking on what the crematoria of Europe have failed to digest.

We have the impression that the officialdom which feeds and clothes us is of the opinion that it is providing presents and that we are living at other people's expense. The property and the money of which the Nazis have robbed us and the millions who have been killed would finance all the western organisations for relief and rehabilitation and there would still be a huge fortune left over.

— We are all in favour of helping ourselves. Our central committees, our newspapers, our camp administrations, our hospitals, schools and nursery schools are proof of it, and so are our artists, our orchestras and our workshops. All these things have grown out of our own endeavours in spite of the many and sometimes almost insuperable difficulties. We want to mobilise what little strength we have and exploit it to the full for the sake of developing this self-help in preparation for a new life.

✡ *All the services indispensable to the maintenance of the life, health, order and welfare of any normal town are performed exclusively by camp residents, not merely because it is expected of them or out of necessity, but out of a sense of personal, social responsibility, a moral regard for work, and the normal drive to develop one's skills and talents for a better future.*

✡ *These young Jews not only want to work, they want to learn a profession and receive vocational training. However, there is a definite aversion to doing any work that might aid the German economy. Work in Germany brings memories of their years of slave labour. Hundreds of groups of young people training for settlement*

2*

in Palestine have been organised, some of them as agricultural units, others are of a vocational training character.

✡   *Each 'kibbutz' has its own quarters in the camp, and its own mess, and operates under a scheduled regimen combining schooling and assigned work. The leaders of the 'kibbutzim' are themselves young people out of the concentration camps, who serve, in effect, as fathers and mothers to groups of children and adolescents ranging in numbers from 50 to 250.*

These youngsters have for years been without parental influence or schooling of any kind. They are stunted three to four years in physical growth, wise beyond their years, though often illiterate, precocious in some psychological respects and retarded in others, especially in social discipline. The close fraternal bonds of the 'kibbutz' group, and the firm hand of its leaders, are slowly restoring them to normal, as perhaps no other kind of organisation could do. (The various 'kibbutzim' have swept up and recovered thousands of orphaned children from all corners of the continent, from peasant homes, monasteries, city streets, forests.)

To facilitate the processes of re-education, the 'kibbutzim' have adopted boy-scout methods. Marching, with their distinctive khaki shorts and white shirts, their Jewish and 'kibbutz' flags, and their spirited singing, they are one of the most colourful camp sights. And by their discipline, high morality and morale, they act as a steadying influence on the adults.

—   We would like to be able to feel alive again, to be people with a purpose who know what they should do with their lives.

✡   *There are in Germany today peculiar schools, the very existence of which manifests the whole catastrophe of European Jewry. The pupils are Jewish men and women between the ages of 18 and 55 or more, who are learning a trade; they want to leave Germany, and skill and will-power will earn them their emigration. The great majority of the Jews, regardless of age, want to go to Palestine.*

—   After six years we are again sitting on school benches. In front of us are books. Lecturers are addressing us in the same language, in which only a short while ago the liquidation of the ghettos was proclaimed, in the same language, in which time was beaten for the death marches in the concentration camps: *links, zwei, drei, vier, links* . . . Now the language sounds different to us. It provides us with the knowledge for which we have been craving during the six lean years.

And we all endeavour to be good pupils. We change step to keep pace with the world which continues to make progress. But sometimes we lose the rhythm and hear—but only for a moment —instead of a chemical formula a dull echo: *links, zwei, drei, vier* . . .

You have to shut your eyes tightly and swallow a bitter taste and . . . carry on. We have to carry on. Behind the barbed wire, in the labour battalions, we have become tough. Most people have no idea how hard it is to sit on a school bench after what we have been through, to take an interest in chemical formulae and theorems. Each one of them has been put to some use or other: in the construction of aeroplanes, in the injection of poison, in the modernisation of the furnaces for cremation.

Nevertheless we are studying. Or perhaps because of all this. Because knowledge is power. Knowledge and compassion create the power to love which we need. This power which will have nothing to do with destruction, with murder and torture, this power of construction we want to serve to the best of our abilities. With this power we will rebuild our ruined lives and the future of the Jewish people.

✡ *Those with religious inclination, given a proper atmosphere, are quickly and thoroughly rehabilitated. Religion and Zionism— these are the only two ideas which bring hope and vitality to survivors in the camps. It can be stated, without exaggeration, that all other ideas and ideals once popular in some Jewish quarters (socialism, communism) have disappeared.*

✡ *No Jewish DP-camp is without a synagogue and the other facilities required by religious Jews. Every camp has a kosher kitchen today. All the larger camps have officiating rabbis. The Jewish DP's have turned their camps into small Jewish communities with all the regular facilities and institutions so characteristic of a Jewish community in Eastern Europe.*

✡ *I found that the religious Jews in the camps were relatively happy. It was apparent that they have a deep faith, in spite of the hell of suffering which they have gone through. They worry about religious practices, about prayerbooks, about keeping the Sabbath, about kosher meat. It fills up the time of the leaders and gives their adherents the feeling that something is being done for them, and so they are satisfied and grateful. It is bad, they say, but it was worse, and it will be better.*

☼ *Immediately after liberation and physical recovery, these Jews began the painful reconstruction of their lives. Destitute of family in most cases, the first step in the process was the establishment by each of a special patchwork type of kinship group. Incorporated in it, generally, are the few surviving distant kin, former landsmen, and, above all, concentration camp 'brothers'. These relationships are so close and intense that they often provide administrative difficulties when overcrowding requires the redistribution of a group to other rooms or, worse, to other camps.*

☼ *The next major step is the establishment of the family by marriage, early among the single people, relatively late among the widowed. Despite disheartening living conditions, children often follow quickly. Even for a population predominantly young adult, the birthrate is extraordinarily high: children are needed as pillars of a normal life; and the traditional high valuation placed upon children among Jews as a foundation for group survival has been still further heightened by the slaughter of almost an entire generation of Jewish children.*

☼ *Jewish life in Central and Eastern Europe is in chaos. It can be characterised as that of a people uprooted and on the march. In a sense, all the Jews, whether they live in DP-camps or still remain in their countries of origin, could properly be classified as refugees and displaced persons. All of them have been displaced from their homes and cities during the war. Practically all of them have passed through the Nazi labour and concentration camps ... After liberation, some of them returned to their countries and towns of origin, mainly to search for families and homes; others were driven back there by the occupying forces. But they have discovered that all their sacrifices have not made them any more welcome in the lands of their birth. Now they continue in a state of wandering—dispossessed, unsettled, looking for a home. There is a continuous movement of evacuation. Smaller communities have been written off with blood and tears, while others are being closed down and merged with larger ones.*

✡   *The number of Jewish displaced persons in the U.S. zone in September 1945 did not exceed 40,000. The majority had been in concentration camps and had been restored to freedom on German soil. Already then, however, the movement of Jews from Eastern Europe to the west was starting. Thousands of survivors in Poland, Hungary and other countries, the memory of what they had been through fresh in their minds, and the spectre of fresh antisemitic outbursts before them, began the trek westwards in the hope of continuing their way to Palestine.*

✡   *The Nazi legacy is very much alive. The main characteristic of this post-Nazi antisemitism is its violence. The prewar anti-semitic slogans have given way to the new popular slogan 'Jews to the crematoria'. Unlike the prewar variety, antisemitism today begins with murder. More Jews have been murdered in pogroms in Poland, Hungary and Slovakia in these eighteen months than in the entire ten years before the Second World War.*

✡   *The stream of Jewish refugees and displaced persons from Eastern Europe to Germany has very much increased during the past few months. At the end of September, the number of Jews in the American zone of Germany has risen to 140,000. The question of finding accommodation for these displaced persons pending their emigration to Palestine, and the problem of accommodating and educating the large number of children, many of whom are orphans, are both of them difficult to solve.*

✡   *There have been two major waves of Jewish refugees. The first came to the DP-camps from Poland, Hungary, Slovakia, and Carpatho-Ukraine at the end of 1945 and the beginning of 1946. It was the backwash of the illusory chaotic summer return to the countries of origin. It was the first reverse mass movement of dis-illusioned, willing and unwilling repatriates. The second wave came in the summer months of 1946, principally from Poland as the result of mass repatriation of Jewish refugees from the Soviet Union. In both instances the movement of the DP's was spontaneous and un-organised. It took the form of panicky flight, dictated by the series of anti-Jewish pogroms with which the local population greeted the Jewish repatriates. The bloodiest pogrom occurred in Kielce, Poland, on June 4th, 1946, when 43 Jews were murdered and 50 wounded out of a Jewish population of 150.*

✡ *There is no military power which will be able to stop them because the fear of death behind them is much greater than the risk of death before them. The Russian, United States and French military governments realise this fact, and so far have not opposed this illegal movement of Jews from the East to the West.*

✡ *There also arrived in 1946 several hundred Jews who had been expelled from the Sudetenland and from Jugoslavia as Germans, allegedly in retribution for Hitler's crimes. They suffered expulsion with millions of other Germans these liberated countries had expelled, in imitation of the racism of their former enemy. Thus the Jews twice fell victim to racism: first as Jews, then as Germans.*

✡ *In addition to children with families, a large number of unaccompanied children has arrived—orphans whose parents were put to death or died of want in camps in Russia, children saved by non-Jewish families and restored to the Jewish communities. For the most part the children came in organised groups under the leadership of members of various youth movements. Separate children's centres were opened during the summer and autumn of 1946. At present there are 11 centres with a total child population of 3,400. In addition, there are several hundred orphans in various adult assembly centres—most of them in charge of relatives.*

✡ *Of 400 children, most were without shoes, nor had they any other footwear. There was not enough food and the children went hungry. The school was without benches, without a table or any other furniture, and lacked all essentials for carrying out proper instruction. Twenty children went to a kindergarten, where the only item for object lessons was a heap of pebbles. Their teacher was a young girl.*

— Children speaking different languages, at different stages in their education—children who because of our past experiences have never had any formal education at all . . .

✡ *The children's camp in Indersdorf adjoins an allotment belonging to a blacksmith. This blacksmith has fixed an electrified barbed*

*wire fence between his land and the children's camp (ostensibly to
prevent the theft of fruit) without even providing an appropriate
warning notice. When officials of the relief organisation took him to
task, he is supposed to have said that this wire was intended for the
Jewish children. 1947 ... it is two years since the end of the war,
two years since the so-called liberation; for two years Germany has
had a democratic government ...*

*Indersdorf is a camp exclusively for children between the ages of
eight and sixteen; most of them are orphans, some are half-orphans,
still rarer are the children who have a brother or a sister left alive;
to none of them has fate preserved both the parents.*

✵   *It was when I saw the children that I realised fully how great
was the misery. Almost all of them have not nearly enough clothing.
What they do have is old and worn. Their shoes are in need of
repair or worn out or they have no shoes at all. One can see immediately that they are homeless refugees. Many of them no longer
have any parents. The only thing they are guilty of is that they are
Jews. Doubtlessly they are living under the worst conditions of any
children in Europe—including those of our ex-enemies. Many of
them were born while their parents were fleeing—who knows under
what conditions? Some of them have come from Central Asia, where
their parents had taken refuge from the Germans. They don't know
what it's like to have a home, to have a regulated family life; they
have never been happy and they don't know the meaning of peace.*

—   After the great terror we were confronted with the question
of the future; I believe that not one of the Jews in postwar
Germany wanted anything except to get away from there.

✵   *The tragedy of the survivors shows in their eyes: the awful past
and the burning question of the present: when will they be able to
leave and where will they go?*

—   Liquidate Jewish life in Germany, that was the general
solution advocated at that time.

—   I stepped again on to German soil in 1946, probably the
first Jewish civilian to do so, in order to keep the promise which
I had made myself to help the survivors. I saw them and spoke
to them in the DP-camps and occasionally in the towns and

villages, and it seemed to me that there was only one solution: every Jew who survived in Germany had to be helped to leave the country.

— But who wanted them, these starved, sick, destitute Jews?

✡ *More than one hundred thousand East European Jews—most of them are only living for the day on which they will at last be able to leave Germany, for which they have nothing but hatred and contempt. These refugees feel no affinity with the Jewish community in Germany either. They consider that Jews who live in Germany can be no better than the Germans.*

✡ *Between the years 1945 and 1952/53, the Jewish population consisted mainly of displaced persons, because only a few German Jews had survived the catastrophe. But even these last few survivors had had enough. They were deeply disillusioned, they wanted to leave the country in which they had been born, wanted to sever all connection with its people who, even if they were perhaps not personally guilty, had at least become partly responsible . . .*

— It is when we concern ourselves with the problem of our emigration, which has become for many of us, probably for the majority, the most vital question, that we become most painfully aware that our liberation has not been complete. Thanks to the fact that we have regained our rights, we have once more become German citizens—and so we can neither emigrate nor immigrate anywhere.

✡ *Everybody I spoke to wanted to leave Germany, and neverthe-less most of them will remain there for the time being, partly because of the practical difficulties of emigrating, partly because they lack the courage to start again in a foreign country, with a foreign language . . .*

— Emigration is the aim of many, but another solution will have to be found for some, because these people are in their present condition incapable of earning a living abroad.

✡ *Only two groups have the desire to stay in Germany—half-Jews and partners of mixed marriages, most of whom have not gone through the camps and have been spared the worst experiences; they hope, through their families, to find new roots in Germany and also to re-establish themselves economically. There is a second group, a*

*small circle of active politicians of Jewish origin who still believe in
their political mission. Another section, unable to emigrate, are the
aged and infirm who, without relatives, have come back from the
camps mentally and physically broken. They have not the vitality to
think of re-starting their lives somewhere else.*

— It has to be assumed that those who will stay will mostly be
old people, and those members of the community whose connection with Judaism is slight. The children of those who remain
will either emigrate, or else they mostly do not consider themselves Jews, so that the Jewish community cannot count on them.

✡ *They exchanged one type of camp for another and waited for a
final decision concerning their future. The first emigrants left Europe
a year after the end of the war.*

✡ *The final destination is the problem most thought and spoken of
in the camps. The overwhelming majority desire to go to Eretz Israel.
Only a few have other emigration plans and those are individuals
who have close relatives in some of the American countries.*

✡ *The remnant of European Jewry, wandering about in search of
safety and a place where they would be able to start their lives anew,
want more than anything else to come to the shores of Eretz Israel,
where they might finally be able to feel at home.*

✡ *What sustains the DP's and prevents their complete despair and
demoralisation is the hope that soon the time will come for them to
leave, to take their place as free citizens beside their fellow Jews in
their own country.*

— We regard our stay in Germany as so much time wasted;
we regard Germany as the waiting-room for emigration to
Palestine.

✡ *The fact that Palestine is virtually closed to Jewish refugees has
had wide repercussions in the camps and is increasing the despair of
the DP's.*

✡ *The refugees are bitterly disappointed because they are still
waiting for their emigration. Every word they utter makes it obvious
that they are disillusioned and without hope.*

✡ *Two and a half years after their liberation, the survivors from
the concentration camps are still living in camps and waiting to
become free people.*

— We want to get back to life, we don't want to exist on charity, we want to be responsible for ourselves. But for this we need help, especially do we need others to help us reach the position from which we can help ourselves.

— Many of us see emigration as the only way out of our spiritual and practical difficulties. An enervating uncertainty about our future has been part of our fate ever since the rise of the Nazis. Must we be condemned to continued waiting? Must what strength we have left be wasted on bearing these depressing interim troubles, when it could serve to help us reconstruct our lives in a new home country? Abroad, children, brothers and sisters are waiting for the survivors. When will we be allowed to join our nearest, our only relations?

✡ *The letters in which young people speak of feeling threatened and lonely are deeply moving. If it were only old people who wrote like that it would be understandable. Old people cannot forget. But these are young, energetic Jews, who are desperately longing to leave those countries. Their populations have learned nothing at all from the past; they are responsible for their own plight and must find a way of coping with it. But we and our young people are their victims . . .*

— Our young people are perplexed and don't know which way to turn. They are conscious of their own strength but they get so little support and not enough help . . .

✡ *Surrounded by a hostile population which serves to exacerbate old wounds and create new resentments, these people are coming to the end of their emotional tether. Unless the world is prepared immediately to make a place for them, it will drive this handful of survivors to despair and disaster. They all of them have only one wish, to be quit of Europe; most of them have a compelling desire to emigrate to Palestine.*

✡ *Most of these Jewish refugees came from Russia and had understandable psychological reasons for not wishing to remain in Poland. 'We want not cemeteries but a homeland,' was the slogan with which they came to Germany. They hoped that Germany would be merely the bridge towards the realisation of their dream. Today we know that thousands of Jews found legal and illegal ways to reach*

Palestine. The official figures of the Jewish Agency show that between 15th May 1948 and 31st December 1949, 345,160 Jews immigrated into Israel.

✡   *The thousands of the summer exodus of 1948 became the tens of thousands of the winter of 1949. Between 15th May and 31st October, over 11,000 persons left; in November, 5,300; in December, more than 6,000. The population in Germany, both in and outside the camps, had dwindled to 83,000.*

—   The problem of the emigration of the Jewish refugees has been almost completely solved—without any effort on the part of the Germans.

IV

THE INHERITANCE

✡ *This is the end of the history of German Jewry. (Leo Baeck)*
— But people don't experience their own existence as history.
✡ *We must not and we cannot forget what has happened. But we and the generations who will come after us have to live.*

I am not forgetting what they have done to us as a people. For the sake of the victims we must not forget. But if a new beginning is to be made, I shall not refuse my hand. I have many friends among the Germans.

Let us think of future generations. And we must not forget: the martyrdom has been shared by Jews and . . . many devout Christians. Together we were in the concentration camps . . . Are not ten just men sufficient?

The Jewish spirit in Germany has always been lonely; the Jews have always looked questioningly to their fellow men, and have never received an answer. A new time will come, because such an earth-quake is bound to be the beginning of a new development.

. . . that the new era will provide an answer for the questing Jewish spirit and that this small example will one day grow into an honest co-operation. (Leo Baeck)

— It was never taken for granted that an organised Jewish community would continue to exist in Germany after 1945. Many people all over the world held the opinion that Jews should no longer reside in Germany after the catastrophe of the past years. The comparison with Spain was obvious. Shortly before its downfall, at the time of the inquisition, the Spanish Empire drove its Jews into exile. They did not return there for several centuries.

✡ *Practically everybody agrees that it will be impossible for any Jewish displaced person to remain in Germany for any length of time. Moreover, only a few believe that there is any hope of re-establishing there the pitifully small number of surviving native Jews. The principal reason is the lack of any real change in the attitude of the local population towards the Jews—the absence of any feeling of repentance or guilt. Beneath the surface of an ill-concealed in-difference, antisemitism remains deeply rooted. The remnants of European Jewry remind the local population of too many too horrible crimes, to be either liked or even tolerated.*

✡ *At the sight of the Jews the Germans are reminded of the persecution, which troubles their conscience and which they would rather not know about.*

✡ *The Germans are afraid that their country, cleared of its Jews by the Nazis, will once again be overrun by Jews from the East.*

✡ *Anyone working in Germany even for only a short time will be left in no doubt about the deep and secret hatred and hostility which the Jews still arouse in every area of German life. It will take years, perhaps generations, before this virulent form of antisemitism has been exhausted in Germany.*

✡ *The Jews are by no means part of the German people today. True, there are the links between Jews and Gentiles. Yet the forcible separation, which had been effected by the Nazi decrees, was not removed at the time of the liberation.*

✡ *. . . that now that the synagogues and all traces of Jewish life have been destroyed, no attempt should be made to recreate Jewish life and so give rise to the possibility of a repetition of past events.*

✡ *Germany is no place for Jews.*

✡ *To the Jews from Germany their former country is the grave-yard of their families. There are no bonds left between them and Germany.*

✡ *According to the opinion of most of its Jewish contemporaries abroad, German Jewry, seen historically, has been made obsolete by its own past.*

✡ *Why create new day-dreams of a new German-Jewish symbiosis? It could bring about a situation which would encourage wishful thinkers to regard Germany as a safe harbour.*

— Others advise us to persevere, to play our part in educating the German people in democracy for the sake not only of the

Jews but of the world. They overlook that many of us will
remain here quite simply because we are Germans.
— The Jews of the world have decided to have nothing more to
do with Germany—to us this seems to be a final victory for Hitler.
— No Hitler can deny us our homeland.
— Should a Jewish position be given up just because Hitler
wanted it that way?
— If in future there are to be no Jews in Germany, we will
merely have brought about of our own accord what Hitler wanted.
— The Jewish people does not take its bearings by the experiences of a few decades, but thinks in centuries.
— There seems to be no political and no moral justification for
wanting to turn the Jewish remnant in Germany into the
'untouchables' of the Jewish people . . . to impose upon them in
addition to their past sufferings the stamp of the leper.
— I don't know whether to call this attitude fanatic or malicious.
— Jewish antigermanism.
— In the beginning there were some who attacked the Nazis
less than they attacked the German Jews—they attacked them
as short-sighted because they wanted to remain in Germany.
— Not only our enemies wanted to liquidate the Jewish community; many of our friends were against the continuing existence of Jewish communities in Germany.
— A negative attitude contributes nothing to a solution. Our
positive attitude has these two advantages: it is frank and
generous towards the Germans and it allows us to act according
to the demands of the profoundest teachings of our religion.
— . . . that to separate, as morally defective, one or another of
the nations from the community of peoples, is contrary to the
spirit of Jewish teachings and of Jewish tradition.
— If political or moral reasons made it impossible for an
organised Jewish community to exist in Germany one would
obviously have to draw the necessary conclusions.
† *The crucial test for German democracy is the treatment of its
Jews. (John McCloy, American High Commissioner)*
— The existence of Jewish communities—however small—in
Germany is vital. How these communities will fare will enable

the rest of the world to measure the progress of Germany's democratic development.

✡ *If there are no Jews here, Germany will be lacking a voice that will persistently demand things that should be demanded of Germany.*

— ... that the world's intentions towards Germany and its opinion of it will always depend upon Germany's attitude to the Jewish question.

— It will be a criterion for the rest of the world whether or not Germany is capable of establishing a healthy relationship with its Jewish communities.

† *The fate of those who have been persecuted is the mirror of the future fate of the German people.*

† *We were poorer without them, and we shall be poorer still if we drive them out—drive them out by not endeavouring to make them stay.*

† *It is a strange fate for us, that while we had Jewish citizens we were a great power, and when we tried to destroy them we destroyed ourselves.*

— I went to Dr. Kurt Schumacher, who spent twelve years in prison and concentration camps, suffering the same fate as our own people. And when I asked him: 'Do you think that all the Jews should leave Germany?' his answer to me was that the presence of Jews was essential for the salvation of the rising German generation and the re-education of all those who, voluntarily or involuntarily, had served the forces of inhumanity. And for the first time he pronounced the thesis that to clear Germany of its Jews would be to act in agreement with Hitler.

— And you must not forget, my friends, that 1·2 million German non-Jews, who were Hitler's opponents between 1933 and 1945, languished in the concentration camps, or were killed, or shot while trying to escape.

— We will know how to keep faith with these Germans.

✡ *They encounter Germans of whom they know that they did not betray their own humanity. And there are many Germans who did not turn against the Jews, many who protected them even under the most difficult circumstances, who risked their own lives to feed them. They should be remembered.*

— And we must try to understand that many Germans would have liked to help but were helpless, were prevented by the terror which stalked through every apartment, into every room . . .

— We must not carry our suspicions so far that we reject people who would like to co-operate with us merely because they did not actively oppose the Nazi regime. Not everybody can be a hero.

— As a German citizen of Jewish faith I am on the side of the decent Germans.

— People often talk about Jewish optimism. This attitude of mind ought not to be confused with that which refuses to acknowledge experiences. The world did not begin only yesterday, not even in Germany.

✡ *On this question of being German and being Jewish—try to be a little less damaging. (Franz Rosenzweig)*

— We have survived the catastrophe—if our survival is to have any meaning it must be the origin not merely of rights for us but also of solemn obligations.

— The jack-boots of the Gestapo have trampled on half of Europe and destroyed all Jewish life; they have not destroyed the spiritual and cultural values of our community.

— . . . how essential it is that some understanding should be shown for the Jews who are living in Germany. They have a mission to fulfil; perhaps it will take a long time for others to realise its value and extent.

— Ought we to turn our backs on Germany and its people in memory of our dead? Ought we not to forgive and dare to try once more to make our moral and cultural values available to our surroundings, in spite of the fact that they have been rejected once? That is the decisive question, and perhaps that is an obligation which history has laid upon the Jews as a consequence of the catastrophe.

— Soon after the end of the war I returned to Berlin, which had been my home town, to look for survivors and enquire about the fate of those who had disappeared. After all that had happened, an attempt was being made to renew Jewish life on the same soil, amongst the same people, who may have looked away or looked on or perhaps even have taken an active part—who could tell? Everything that was Jewish in me rebelled against this attempt, but I could not agree with those who considered it a sort of patriotic (Israeli) duty to indulge in feelings of hatred against the Jews who remained in Germany. I had many heated discussions at the time . . . and reached the conclusion, that the words of the late Chief Rabbi Kook indicated the right direction. He used to say: 'Better a little unjustified love for our fellow men than much unjustified hatred.'

† *To show love—does that require courage? Certainly! Hatred is a consequence of the heart's indolence, it is cheap and easy. Love is always a risk. But we have to take risks if we want to gain anything. (Theodor Heuss)*

† *Reconciliation does not mean that we have to compromise with our conception of the truth; it means a feeling of brotherhood which takes everything into account.*

— This is our country, we belong to it, we love it, we feel that it is our responsibility, too.

✡ *The Jews have adapted themselves more closely to the Germans than to any other people; one could almost say that they have identified themselves with them. In no other language are European Jews so much at home as in German—one talks of language and means culture.*

✡ *Probably, the Jews achieved a greater measure of creative assimilation in Germany than in any other country. Since the emancipation, their contribution to the cultural and economic life of Western Europe was greater in Germany than anywhere else. And German culture more than any other has influenced the modern Jewish culture, both Yiddish and Hebrew, of Eastern Europe. (Nahum Goldmann)*

— The Jews have never attempted to protect themselves from Germany and German influences; their defences have always been intended only against Christianity . . .

— We Jews look back with gratitude, sometimes to our own hurt. Already the law of Moses stipulates that we should remember even the sojourn in Egypt without hatred, because although we were helpless and oppressed slaves, still we had dwelled in that country.

† *We know ourselves insolubly united especially with those Jews who were like us born in Germany. We cannot imagine a past from which their contribution is lacking.*

† *The only new element is an awareness of a specially close connection between the fate of the Jews and that of the Germans.*

† *Apart from the Romans, who destroyed Jerusalem and caused the dispersion of the Jews all over world, no other people has so insolubly and so tragically linked its own fate to that of the Jews as we have done.*

— One talks of Christians and Jews in Germany, loosely, out of habit or mental laziness, often for political reasons and sometimes with bad intentions. But that is wrong—there lived in Germany Jews of German origin and Gentiles of German origin. They may have been good and bad in different ways. But they were more than related . . . they were alike, because they had been shaped by the same soil, the same sun, the same fields and forests and the same culture.

— If I could no longer be at home in my native land, I would not wish to be at home anywhere else; one cannot have more than one home. The German language, German culture, German literature, German music, German philosophy and my German friends would remain the basis of my existence.

— Anyone who contests my claim to Germany contests my right to think and speak in my native language, to breathe my native air: and so I have to defend myself against him as if he wanted to kill me.

✡ *If life were ever to put me to the torture and tear me apart, indeed I know which part would have my heart which after all is not situated in the middle; I also know that I would not survive such an operation. (Franz Rosenzweig)*

✡ *German by emotion. (Martin Buber)*

✡ *We believe that the day will come when Germany's history and the history of the Jews will no longer be two separate stories, but one history will again apply to us all. (Alfred Hirschberg, 1935)*

✡ *The 'new beginning' continued an existence interrupted by*

Hitler and by exile. The majority of former German Jews who had emigrated found this attitude incomprehensible.

— Antisemitism has not been able to destroy this relationship. Presumably not even when the distance in space amounts to thousands of miles. There is a mystery at work here, which can be described but not explained. Many of us remained here, not in the hope of getting something out of it, which is a malicious interpretation, but because of this mysterious relationship. It might make some of our enemies uncomfortable, nevertheless it has to be said—there is such a thing as a feeling of gratitude, for instance to those Germans who have been our companions since we were young, let us say Mozart and Beethoven, Goethe and Kant. There are obligations here which cannot be got rid of. Amongst these spiritual assets is also the love for one's native country, which cannot be constricted by any laws.

✡ *A relationship with centuries of history is not easy to dissolve. We have acknowledged that we belong to the Jewish people but this has never meant that we could surrender our German culture . . . Thousands of German Jews have been brought up as Germans . . . Years, decades will pass and we know that generations to come will cherish the German culture which they have received.*

— . . . that we are not bad Jews, although we think of ourselves as good and true Germans: we have received our education in German schools, we have listened to the interpretation of God's word in German out of the mouth of our Jewish rabbi and will continue to listen to it, and we are not ashamed to think that Germany is our native country and that the German language is our mother tongue. I and people like me have remained in Germany because we did not want to leave it, because we would not permit any fool and maniac who deceived Germany to deprive us of our native land.

Do only the last twelve years of Germany's existence count?

It is easy to turn our backs now that the country has been defeated, after it has been maintained officially for a few years that we are not German citizens. But those who maintained this are no longer in power. We ought to take care that we ourselves do not foster and perpetuate their criminal ideology and intolerance.

We are not homeless refugees, neither do we subscribe to the Zionist point of view, we acknowledge that we are German citizens; we reject every theory of racial primacy and uphold the faith and ethics of our fathers. We belong here because we were born here, to this language, this culture, this way of life; we insist that living and working here does not prevent us from being good Jews. We belong here all the more now that our native land is weak and defeated, whether through its own or anyone else's fault does not matter . . . To remain is our contribution towards the re-education of German youth.

— This is the country in which we have grown up, whose culture we have made our own, to which we have a personal relationship—we share the responsibility for its fate, not altogether voluntarily. Although we were state enemies No. 1, and carry the physical and mental scars to prove it, the allied powers have passed laws to reinstate us as German citizens. We are anxious about the future, and not only our own.

— We have repeatedly expressed the wish to contribute to the rebuilding of Germany, in spite of everything that has happened. We are Germans and join the ranks of other Germans, who take Kant, Goethe, Schiller and Lessing as their example. We want to help Germany to regain its standing as a civilised state. We want to help to re-establish the rule of law . . . We will not let anyone dissuade us from our path and from our aims. It needs a constant effort to bring oneself to forgive, and to forgive again . . .

— The relationship between Jews and non-Jews in Germany has been destroyed to the core; that it will redevelop of its own accord is too much to expect. To re-create a normal relationship between Jews and non-Jews in Germany in the foreseeable future will require a consciously directed, to some extent artificial effort. We must foster gently what this monstrous decade has destroyed.

— Jewish people who have returned live in isolation and feel lonely, because the bridge to the 'fellow Germans' has yet to be reconstructed. The mind refuses to understand what has happened, the heart rejects it, the Jews cannot come to terms with it and they will never again be light of heart; but that does not mean that they have to withdraw so to speak into a corner of life, unable to contribute to the present and the future.

— After all that has happened to Jews in this country, it will certainly be difficult for many of us to be good Germans.

— I have the impression that the German people will never again accept the Jews into equal partnership. I have lost touch completely with all the friends I had in pre-war days. We have become such strangers to each other, I believe that for Jews life in Germany will never again be what it was before Hitler.

— The fate of the Jews in Germany today is, above all, loneliness. Many are the sole survivors of large families and wide circles of friends. Other families have survived the persecution and the war, but have been scattered all over the world. The individual is often no more than a fragment of a unit which has been destroyed. The connection with the German people has been severed; the Jews here live in an atmosphere of cold indifference, often of something much worse. German Jewry as a whole has difficulties in its relationship with the Jews of the world. The Jew in Germany must say a prayer: Turn towards me and have mercy, for I am poor and lonely.

— . . . that the shadow of the past will fall across any reconstruction. A more important aspect: people have to come to terms with the present, with their state of mind.

— This atmosphere, a strange mixture of bad conscience and good intentions . . .

— Both Germans and Jews have suffered and been without hope; from this shared experience there may grow a shared hope, a common future.

— The occupying powers have reinstated us as German citizens —and so given us a share in the responsibility for Germany's fate. Whether we like it or not!

— But this warning must be given: with the decision to remain in Germany the Jews there will link their fate to that of the German people. Together with them they will have to bear the memory of the past and endeavour to rebuild the country; they will have to share the consequences of Germany's guilt.

— Not we but life has decided that Jewish communities continue to exist in Germany.

— ... not only for the benefit of the Jews in Germany, but beyond that for the sake of the whole Jewish and non-Jewish world—always fully aware that we are of minor importance.

— To keep alive the great tradition of German Jewry—there is not a single reason to suppose that this dream could ever be realised.

— Whatever positive achievements may be arrived at will be a triumph of life over the realm of death.

— We are few, but much depends on us.

— ... to prove to people abroad that we have remained strong in spite of everything; to prove to the Jews of the world that the Jews in Germany have kept faith with themselves.

— ... consider today and tomorrow and leave the day after tomorrow to Him who is wiser than man.

Whether there will be a German Jewry in the future? That question we cannot answer. But this we know: in the whole history of the Jews the realists have always been those who believed in miracles.

v

A NEW BEGINNING

✡ *In 1945 there remained in Germany about 15,000 German Jews; nearly 300,000 had emigrated, about 170,000 had been killed. The few who had survived in Germany belonged neither to the religious nor to the spiritual nor to the scholarly elite of German Jewry. They founded new Jewish communities . . .*

✡ *Where life is growing death is diminished. (Martin Buber)*

— It is entirely in accordance with a Jewish attitude to life to consider the beginning and above all the act of beginning more important than the ending.

— We are faced here as everywhere in Germany with a fragment of a community.

— Our community is a community of mourners.

✡ *Cemetery communities.*

✡ *We have not the time either to rejoice or to mourn. (Heinrich Heine)*

— The Jewish communities in Germany today exist to shelter the remnant who has survived the catastrophe.

— Our community is intended to provide Jewish people with a little home ground.

— The time from May 1945 until autumn 1946 may roughly be considered to be the period when the new communities were founded.

✡ *The founders of the Jewish communities which were re-established after the war were Jews who had survived the persecution because they were closely related to the German people.*

✡ *The founders and the members of the new communities belonged overwhelmingly to those German Jews who had arrived at the end of a natural and passive process of assimilation, the symptoms of which were a personal and public dissociation from Judaism, showing most clearly in the withdrawal from the congregations, in baptism and in mixed marriages. They almost all stood on the periphery of Judaism* . . .

— By far the greater number of surviving Jews were partners of mixed marriages, that is to say Jews who mostly lived on the fringe of Judaism, but most of them showed an unmistakable desire to continue of their own accord an association forced upon them by the Nazis. The years of the persecution had left deep impressions and made many painfully aware of being Jews. Besides a feeling of gratitude, there was also the almost proud satisfaction which those who had been persecuted felt towards their former oppressors; they wanted to remain a group apart.

— The founders of the new communities were mostly beyond middle-age; their life must have seemed to them in many ways a failure and they drew confidence for it from the idea of rebuilding the communities. Because of their age and past history, but also in view of the immediate practical needs which had to be satisfied, the Jewish community was best suited to express their new optimism. It was a very good instrument for reinforcing their religious and social obligations, and for sustaining a group which had been completely deprived of all sense of security.

✡ *To these members of the German-Jewish remnant, with their deep-seated if repressed identification with Germany, the reconstruction of the Jewish communities must have been a substitute for the reconstruction of their native Germany.*

— Within a few hours or days after the end of the war, in the midst of the still smoking ruins of the devastated cities, these old-new communities were resurrected, with insufficient resources, by men who perhaps had not entered a synagogue since their bar-mitzvah and whose helpers were married to Gentiles.

All these men were driven by one desire. In that chaos, they wanted to save what was not yet beyond saving, and to give what help they could, and in most cases they made it their first task to arrange divine services, as Jews returning from exile have always done.

✡ *Although the entry of the allied armies saved the Jews from further persecution, it did not mean that they could then resume their former lives as though nothing had happened. Antisemitic*

incidents in the first few months after the war, a lack of co-operation
and restitution, the mental and physical solitude in which most of the
Jews found themselves . . .

— We have been liberated and can make a new beginning, and
only now do we realise how completely we have lost our bearings.
We cannot take up our lives at the point where they were interrupted by the Nazis because that point has vanished. We have to
look for a new point at which to begin, right at the beginning
again; we have to get used to things. And it will be especially
difficult for us to begin again, because under the strain of the
persecution we have lost a great deal of our vitality, because we
have grown older, not only older in years but beyond the years,
because we are sick and weak. Suddenly and without transition
we are released from the isolation in which we were kept for
years and put back into our surroundings, to which we have
become strangers and which have become strange to us. The
consequence of all this is that we still do not feel completely free,
that we don't yet know what to do with our freedom.

Certainly, it is very nice that we should be granted some
social assistance, that an attempt should be made to provide us
with money and with food. But this is not the way to bring about
a definite solution, it only serves to disguise the problem and the
result is to make us feel even more dissatisfied and disappointed
than we feel anyway. Many of us are still too young to retire, to
live on patronage and charity. We want to work, we want to do
things, we want to be self-supporting. What we ask of others is
that they should make this possible for us.

— The majority of us are no better off now than we were before
the liberation. Certainly, we are no longer under pressure from
the Gestapo, the persecution which we have suffered is a thing of
the past; but does this mean that we are now all right? We don't
want to deny that it is partly our own fault. It is not very easy for
us to adjust ourselves. We had lost our independence, we had
forgotten what it means to be free. Our former circle of friends
and relations would have provided us with sympathy and support, but it no longer exists. During the time of our seclusion,
Germany and its people have become strangers to us. To people

3

abroad we are Germans, who must share the fate intended for the German people in consideration of its past. But inside Germany we are aliens, who can't adjust and who are regarded as aliens.

— We have grown older, our attitude to life has changed and our surroundings have changed as well; conditions and circumstances are new and different. Our relations have been exterminated, we have lost our friends, our former connections no longer exist. For many of us this is only a provisional life. But it must not and cannot remain provisional for long. We have waited far too long already for the time when we might return to normal living conditions.

— We are once more free people. The relief organisations from abroad have started to function, and the exodus has begun. The fact that we have been victims has at last been officially recognised, and we are receiving practical aid. Again and again we have to fight for things which are essential for daily life. No decision has yet been reached on the question of making reparations. Our property has not yet been returned to us. We are continually confronted with the spirit of the past, which refuses to be conquered entirely and everywhere. True, we have been recognised as people with equal rights, but our equality is often only theoretical.

Certainly, symbolic achievements cannot alleviate the misery which is greater in our community than in any other part of the population. It should be remembered that all of us have been persecuted; our way of life has been destroyed and economically we are completely ruined.

✡ *In the last few months, the life of the Jews has been fundamentally changed by giving them the status of 'victims of fascism'. It was by no means easy to achieve this status which seems to us so self-evident. 'Jews,' they were told, 'we don't know any Jews. We only know human beings. For us all human beings are equal. We don't want any privileges for Jews. That would only create more prejudice.' On their recognition as 'victims of fascism' depended whether the emaciated and half-starved Jewish remnant would survive the winter, or not.*

What does the new status imply? It entitles them to additional rations of potatoes, vegetables and jam and includes also the

'*Aryan*' *partners of mixed marriages who, in many cases, had starved themselves in order to get some additional food for their children, their husbands or their wives.*

— The relief granted to the 'victims of fascism' has little effect and can on no account be considered adequate. That Jews are allocated one increment means that half of them, who because of their age or the state of their health are unfit for work, receive grade three ration-cards. This is insufficient to maintain people who have been starved for years. The consequences would be catastrophic if we did not receive food-parcels from abroad.

— The majority of us are today no better off than we were on the day of our return. So far, we have received nothing of our former property, which the Hitler regime stole from us to the gain of quite a few Germans. We exist on charity. Many call themselves lucky to possess a suit and a pair of shoes, and there are people who don't even possess that much. War-damaged rooms which don't keep out the weather have become our homes, and we live in daily fear of being deprived of even these make-shift shelters in favour of the returning denazified party members. We have a few sticks of furniture, not that we can call them our own ... Some Jews who have returned don't even have a bed or a chair, since the relief organisations cannot help everybody. Up till now, the Germans have not even tried to make available to us the flats and houses which once belonged to Jews.

— A great number of Jews are inadequately housed. There is a shortage of furniture and the necessary household utensils. There is a very great shortage of clothing and shoes. The Jews have no income, there is no work for them, they have to rely on public assistance, and that is our greatest problem. Another problem is our religious life. We have neither a synagogue nor ritual objects or prayerbooks, we don't even have a rabbi.

— Those who sought our help were almost without exception physically and emotionally completely exhausted. It was not a question of completing some paperwork, it was a question of providing these survivors of the holocaust with the hope that things would soon be different for them. Many of them were so close to death, that all there was time for was to comfort them with at least the illusion of a solution to their problems as a final act of mercy.

— We know very well that the interests of our tiny minority must appear insignificant compared with the problems which bedevil world politics. But the individual possesses only a short span of life, and we have been deprived of too much of our time and energy already.

— Would it not have been better for us if we had shared the fate of our relations who committed suicide or died in the gas chambers?

— The past year has been a year of high hopes and shattering disappointments for the survivors. And future historians will one day call this the year of the liberation of the Jews . . .

— We have just lived through an exceptionally cold spell, which has had catastrophic effects because of the fuel shortage. The emergency was so great that the German authorities concerned appealed to the Allies for help for the German population; one can imagine what such an emergency means for the surviving Jews. For many years we did not receive even the basic rations essential for maintaining life, and our health has been seriously and permanently affected. Half the Jewish population of Berlin is above 50 years old and for this reason alone is not capable of providing for itself. Especially the old and sick who are the sole survivors of their families were completely helpless in the emergency.

— Nearly 1,800 members of our community are more than 60 years old. Of these, it has been possible to accommodate only a small percentage in the old people's homes which belong to the Berlin Jewish community; the majority—about 1,600—do not live in an institution. Their homes consist of makeshift rooms which are barely furnished and cannot be properly heated. They live by themselves and are without relatives who might look after them. Many of these people are also sick and handicapped. During the time of the persecution their health has suffered. They are especially hard hit by the excessive cold; they don't have enough warm clothing and they have trouble in collecting their allocation of food and fuel. There is an immediate danger that many of them will be destroyed by the everyday difficulties with which they cannot cope.

— Anyone who has watched the distribution of meals to the old and sick will have been shocked by the sight. They are all of them emaciated and bear the traces of these past fourteen years clearly enough.

. . . will be able to form an impression of the emergency situation which still exists amongst the Jews here today, almost two years after the war, so that the survivors are by no means out of danger, on the contrary, the danger threatening them grows every day.

— We have in Berlin 20 Jewish children who have survived the concentration camps; as babies and toddlers they were treated like criminals, they were exposed to hunger, cold, vermin and contagious diseases . . . All of them have repeatedly been seriously ill; most of them will never be completely healthy and they will never be the same as other children.

For years they have suffered starvation and the effect which this has had on their health could only be made good through very special care within the next few years. German children were still receiving an adequate diet when Jewish mothers were desperate for a crust of bread . . . Since the end of the war there has been a general shortage, under which Jewish children have suffered together with everyone else. They have grown up in an atmosphere of fear, misery, want and hunger; they are still living in wretched circumstances today.

— The Jews in Berlin are desperately in need of help, while the welfare department can only alleviate the worst of the misery.

— Who will deny that we are in need of help! We are in need of help because nobody understands our problems and nobody cares; we are in need of help because the spectre of postwar Europe, hunger, does not spare our ranks. Certainly, your relief organisations have done a lot of work, and individual Jews abroad have been ready to help us. Much has been done. But not enough, because we are confronted with so much plain misery.

— We have spent some days travelling across Berlin, and we would never have thought it possible that there could be so much poverty and misery amongst the Jews . . . and this in the second winter after our liberation.

— People reproach us for being reserved and for not making an effort to adapt ourselves. After the fall of Berlin there was hardly one of us who did not wish to play his part in rebuilding Germany. But after you have offered yourself repeatedly in vain, you finally feel a little undignified . . . Apart from this it has to be stated quite clearly that it is not we who have to adapt but other people, or else we will retrospectively become fellow-travellers.

— We Jews would have liked to have finished with the past. We have offered our hand in reconciliation. It has been refused. Already in August 1945 we wrote to the military administration that only those who were really guilty should be brought before the courts to be sentenced, and that unimportant people and fellow-travellers should be given the benefit of the doubt. If we had been interested in revenge our attitude would have been different. But as time passes we become more and more embittered, because we cannot help seeing that the Germans have refused to learn their lesson. And this makes us feel sorry, because after all we belong to this country, it is our home.

— And how did we revenge ourselves? The teaching which has been part of our heritage since biblical times commands us to treat kindly and with care those who have been hurt, and confronted with the colossal German catastrophe we instinctively adopted this attitude. Our experiences of the last two years have proved quite clearly that, in spite of what has been said by numerous people both in their official and private capacities, the Germans have little or no intention of acknowledging the obligation they have towards the surviving Jews to make some sort of reparations . . .

— The Jews returned from the concentration camps without hatred, which surely they had been given sufficient cause to feel. In spite of their impaired health, the majority of them were willing to serve the new democratic Germany. They undertook to act as mediators between Germany and the world. The Germans ought to show them a little more gratitude . . .

— We are horrified to realise that thousands and tens of thousands of Germans have not changed at all. In 1945, when we returned from the concentration camps, we willingly offered our hands to anyone whose own hands were clean, to all those whom we considered decent Germans. We wanted them to have the opportunity to make amends. That was two years ago, and we are still waiting for a spark of common decency . . .

— In the beginning we were optimists and expected justice, but by now we have become very sceptical. After the collapse of the Hitler regime, the force of circumstances caused a few official concessions, but today people don't want to hear any more about the sufferings of the Jews in Nazi Germany and the general attitude is that what has been done is enough to pass for justice.

— Every day it happens that our people are treated with suspicion, indeed even with open hostility, because of the concessions which have been made to them, and they really don't amount to very much. These concessions mean that we are issued with ration cards entitling us to one increment, that we occasionally receive small special allocations and once a month a parcel from a relief organisation abroad. And that is supposed to compensate us for the disadvantages from which we have suffered for years?

✡ *It becomes more and more clear to me that it is far easier for people to live with the six million dead than with a few thousand survivors.*

† *The Nazi indoctrination lasted for twelve years—it cannot be annulled within two.*

† *I now have to plead for understanding for a people who immediately after the war had to work very hard in order to ensure its survival. The Nuremberg trials did not arouse as much interest among the population of devastated Germany as a few pounds of potatoes or a little fuel—the Nazi leaders had never been that popular. (Willy Brandt)*

— Some people were optimists enough to believe that immediately after the war the Germans themselves would organise a movement which, by advocating that reparations, as far as possible, ought to be made, would at least attempt to prove that they realised that the persecution of the Jews had been wrong. These optimists were disappointed and remain disappointed until this day, two years after the end of the war.

— No movement arose in Germany to concern itself with the question of how these people, who had from first till last been the victims of the Nazi regime, were to provide homes and re-establish normal conditions for themselves. No one in Germany took the initiative.

— We don't want charity, we want compensation for the wrong that was done to us. It is time to stop the collections for us, it is time to return to us everything that has been taken away. That is all we want and no more. But we don't want any Nazi to have the impression that by making some contribution he can buy himself out.

— We don't want people to feel sorry for us, we don't want charity, all we want is that people should return what belongs to us, what they have taken away. We want the German people as a whole and each individual within it to act fairly.

— ... and so we are not moved by thoughts of hatred and revenge, but by the thought of justice. We don't want to ask excessive sacrifices from decent Germans and from those who tried to help us even when this endangered their own lives. But many have profited at our expense under the Nazi regime and we demand that their unearned profits should be taken away from them and be used to undo a little of the damage they have done.

— They can dismiss from their minds what they have been told. But our experiences will remain with us always. We left our strength and our health in the camps—nobody can do anything about that now. But people make this mistake: they want to feel sorry for us whereas we demand our rights, they want to give us charity whereas we demand reparations.

We do not demand primarily money and assistance but rehabilitation, justice, and to be treated as human beings.

✡ *In November 1947 General Clay proclaimed the restitution law for the American zone. The French followed suit that same month, while the British took their time and did not do so until the summer of 1949. It took still longer to decide upon reparations, which was to compensate people for loss of life, imprisonment and loss of income and therefore concerned a much wider social group.*

— Restitution is remorse made manifest.

— It took three years to pass the restitution law. As the German ministers refused to sign, it became a military law.

✡ *The restitution law did nothing for the bereaved and the crippled, for the survivors of the concentration camps; it was legislation for the benefit of those who had escaped lightly; it did nothing for those whose whose careers had been interrupted, whose capital consisted of an occupation which they could not practise and which was of no use to them in exile, it was legislation for the benefit of those who had been rich; it did nothing for those who had had a few possessions, only for the class of former property-owners, especially for those who had formerly been economically powerful.*

— Legislation had to be brought about by order of the military government, because the Germans were not willing of their own accord to return the stolen property. And many of those who are in possession of things which belong to the Jews are now betraying an even greater hatred, which makes them not merely refuse to return the stolen property to the rightful owner, but behave as if it were their own.

— It is really not important for those who have been persecuted for political, racial or religious reasons, whether or not they receive some money for having been in a concentration camp and perhaps also a few extra rations and a pair of shoes: these people have experienced and put up with much worse things in the past and, hardened as they are, they will manage to come to terms with their present lot. But for the Germans it is of colossal importance for their whole future, whether or not they will manage to make to the Jews reparations which really deserve to be called that.

— Nobody can bring the dead back to life, and the mental and physical sufferings of those who were persecuted cannot be changed into something that did not happen. Nevertheless— material reparations are the only means of making tangible amends for the crimes of the Nazi regime.

✡ *Actually, it is impossible to make reparations. Europe has*

3*

*been left so poor by the war that it does not have the resources to
provide the few Jewish survivors with even modest living conditions
in view of what they have suffered. Every European nation is
threatened with hunger, and so it is believed necessary in the
responsible quarters to limit to a minimum the supplementary rations
for the former victims, although our people have been starving for
six years. But above all, nobody can restore to the victims their lost
mental and physical energy, or their sleepless nights, or their lost
years. And what is far more important, no one on earth can restore
to life the six million Jews who were our parents and children, our
husbands and wives, our brothers and sisters.*

VI

GERMANY'S STEPCHILDREN

☆   *It seems both a paradox and an irony that Germany, which drive its Jewish population either into exile or death, became after the war, under the protection of the victorious allied powers, a sheltering haven for several hundred thousand Jews, the so-called displaced persons.*

☆   *The Jews who had been liberated from the concentration camps seemed condemned to remain in Germany, in Germany of all places —in the country which they had learned to hate more than any other.*

—   Displaced person—a homeless foreigner, a person without passport and without identity papers, in the middle of the 20th century mania for forms of all sorts; a person without family, without money, without connections, without friends. Confined by invisible powers within a country which to him is accursed. How could he consider it anything else than accursed? Those who were twenty or twenty-two when they were liberated in the concentration camps, were fourteen or sixteen years old in 1939, when Poland was occupied and they were sent to a ghetto. The only Germans they encountered were people in uniform, usually in the uniform of the SS. The only Germans they knew were guards, were enemies, whose purpose it was to torture them. In the concentration camps themselves they saw only horror and brutality, never once heard a kind word, and had reason constantly to be afraid. When should these young Jews from Poland, Lithuania or Rumania ever have had the opportunity to get a different, a good impression of Germany?

—   From the beginning the Jewish refugees created a special problem above all through their absolute refusal to co-operate with their German surroundings in any way.

☆   *Whether these Jews lived in or outside the camps, they tended*

*to cut themselves off from the German (and German-Jewish)
communities in what resembled a self-imposed ghetto. This they
considered necessary because of differences in language and culture.
Whether in camps or in towns, the DP's established a social and
cultural life of their own, with their synagogue, schools, hospitals,
kindergartens, press and publishing companies.*

— They are in *status emigrandi*. They feel that they do not
belong here and consider themselves a group apart; they want to
have their own separate existence. This is what makes it impossible to keep them within the law, this is why they do not fit into
German life—irrespective of the past.

✡ *In the first postwar years everyone in Munich knew that in the
Moehlstrasse could be bought such rare goods as cigarettes, coffee,
and food of all sorts from the DP's, whose source of supply was the
relief parcel from abroad. The occupation authorities protected the
DP's from the German police, and soon the DP's became identified
with the black market. Although most of the DP's left the country
at the earliest possible moment, about 10,000 remained in and near
the Moehlstrasse which became a strange new settlement of little
shacks and makeshift stores where practically everything was for
sale.*

*Most of the Moehlstrasse men, uprooted from their former homes,
able to survive only by highly developed toughness, and without
family and community ties, had the understandable view that they
had a moral right to get the best out of life, and especially out of
Germany. Except for the exchange of goods and money, there
was hardly any contact between them and the German population.*

— I too have been in the Moehlstrasse and I ask: if there is a
God, why, after making us suffer so terribly much in the past,
has he punished us with the Moehlstrasse, which is a disgrace to
us before all the world and which must make every decent Jew
blush with shame?

— It is understandable that human beings, who have been
degraded to animals in the concentration camps, sometimes take
it into their head to exact their own personal reparations from the
Germans.

✡ *The most valuable ones, the real pioneers, were the first to leave*

Germany. Those who remained have not improved in the atmosphere in which Jewish DP's in Germany are forced to live.

— For them, it was not a question of acting legally or illegally, but of living or dying. Society had snatched them away from their occupation and their family, stolen their property, thrown them into ghettos and concentration camps, and after their liberation made them no reparations. Their new surroundings treated them as beggars and offered them charity instead of meeting their demands which were legally and certainly morally clearly justified . . . Inevitably, those who wanted to survive learned to make use of their wits and their elbows.

— Those who are generally called DP's are people who at the age of 13 or 14 were put into ghettos, saw their parents killed before their eyes and were then sent to the concentration camps, which did not exactly set them a good example. Now suddenly these people are released . . .

— It ought to be borne in mind that the majority of the DP's are people who were forcibly deprived of a normal existence and who for years had to fight for their mere survival. Thus it is not surprising that they came rather easily into conflict with the law. But this fact, which incidentally applies to only a few of the DP's here and there, has misled people into regarding them generally as morally inferior. Added to this, the majority of the Jewish DP's are Poles, who have remained in the camps because they can neither go back nor can they go anywhere else, and so, many people equate the term DP with Polish Jew. Therefore, Polish Jews are held responsible without further ado whenever the DP's lay themselves open to criticism.

— People who break the law do so as law-breakers and not as Jews.

— We remember from long ago the attitude of well-meaning antisemites, that they have nothing against the German Jews, but only against the Jews from Eastern Europe.

— Many of the DP's have grown up in the concentration camps, where their living conditions and the behaviour of the people were hardly likely to be good for their morals. In this respect as well they are really victims of the persecution.

— Immediately after the end of the war there were in Germany almost 30,000 Jewish displaced persons, who were starving and in need of medical and every other sort of assistance. The 'Joint' organised supplementary meals for the Jewish population both in and outside the camps, created a comprehensive health service and established rehabilitation and convalescent centres. By 1947, refugees from Poland had increased the number of Jews in Germany to more than 175,000, who were accommodated in about 100 DP-camps. From 1946 till 1950, the 'Joint' imported 60 thousand tons of provisions, comprising food, clothing, medicine, etc. It provided 160,000 Jews in and outside the camps with supplementary rations, cared for the education of more than 13,000 children in 200 schools, and supplied 123 workshops with teachers, materials and machines, which provided occupations for 4,150 Jewish workers. 150 institutions which cared for more than 12,000 people received special medical and dental aid. More than 30,000 children were cared for. And what is perhaps most important: the 'Joint' helped 125,000 people to emigrate from Germany to Israel, the U.S.A., Canada and other countries.

— It took five years for the 120,000 Jews in Bavaria to emigrate to Israel, the United States and other countries, five years before the 65 large DP-camps could be closed.

— At the first official census in September 1945, there were 10,000 people in Belsen; in the autumn of 1950 the population there had fallen to below 1,000 (8,000 emigrated to Israel). About a third of those who remained were invalids and so-called hard-core cases. These were transferred to the Upjever camp near Oldenburg.

— The Central Committee of Liberated Jews in the French zone of Germany will be dissolved at the end of February 1951, as only 50 Jewish DP's remain out of a population of 2,500 who were living there in the first few years after the war. There are forty Jews in Constance and theirs is the only Jewish community in the French zone. A third of the Jews who have remained are unable to emigrate because they are either too old or too sick.

— According to plan, the DP-camp Upjever was finally closed

on 13th August 1951. Of the 420 Jews who still remained in the camp, 30 who were sick were transferred to the Jewish hospitals in the American zone. 106 went to Israel, 63 to Australia and Canada, 125 to the United States and 30 went to Norway and Sweden. This leaves just a few, who joined the communities in the British zone.

These 420 were the last of the survivors from the extermination camp Bergen-Belsen.

About 60,000 people passed through Belsen and its successor camp Upjever during the last few years; for most of them Israel has by now become their home.

— Although the DP-camps have now been closed, the problem of the Jews in Germany has not been entirely solved. A sober and realistic assessment of the situation will show that there are hundreds who cannot or will not leave now but may leave soon, and thousands who will unfortunately have no opportunity at all of leaving within the forseeable future.

— Considering that thousands of Jews have passed through Bavaria in the course of their emigration, it is really not surprising that for various reasons a small proportion of them have remained here.

— Perhaps they succeeded in establishing a business and postponed giving it up from year to year; perhaps they married a Gentile to overcome their feelings of loneliness and isolation; perhaps they felt incapable, physically or emotionally, of uprooting themselves yet again. From time to time they promised themselves, their children and their friends, that they would soon be leaving Germany for ever; no doubt they meant it—and still mean it when they say it today.

✡ *Although the bulk of the Jewish DP population had left its German transit camps by 1951, some 12,000 to 15,000 had made it clear in the following ten years that they intended to remain. About 70 per cent acquired German citizenship, and about one out of six (around 2,000) former East European Jewish DP's married a non-Jewish German. In big cities they joined the German Jews in their communities, constituting about 20 per cent of the Berlin and 40 per cent of the Frankfurt community; while smaller communities, mainly in Bavarian towns near their former camps, were predominantly formed by these former immigrants.*

— There were several places which had been without Jews before 1933, where the DP's now established communities.

— After the war, southern Germany became a large reservoir of former concentration camp inmates and refugees, principally East European Jews from Poland. Although in the next few years these spread over the whole country, in southern Germany they continued to be in the majority and so determined the tone of the Jewish communities much more than in northern Germany.

— The DP's from the concentration camps formed the largest single group; most of them had been in Bergen-Belsen, held firm opinions and therefore played a special part.

— On the whole, this group was composed of people who were very much younger, more lively, and who had closer ties with the Jewish religion—in important respects their influence shows clearly in the present Jewish communities.

— With the influx of people who were much closer to Judaism than the surviving German Jews, the character of the new communities became much more Jewish.

— Yiddish expressions which German Jews had once despised now became common usage among the German survivors; people got used to calling each other *chaver* (comrade) and the communities issued their proclamations in both Yiddish and German. The sort of social gatherings popular amongst East European Jews became customary especially on the Sabbath and Jewish Holy Days, and East European Jews became the experts of the communities on all Jewish questions.

— Jews from Poland and Jews from Germany, coming from opposite backgrounds, belong to two such distinctive groups, that when they come together the differences between them will inevitably make themselves felt. If they thought of each other as strangers they would merely notice these differences, but because they are all Jews together they criticise each other. Take for example the Yiddish language. Without having given it much thought, many native German Jews consider the colloquial

Yiddish used by the millions of East European Jews as 'bad German'. On the other hand, many of the Jews from Eastern Europe are just as narrow-minded. They often quite seriously express the opinion that German Jews are not real Jews at all because they speak the language of their German surroundings.

— There is a restlessness amongst the East European Jews which makes it more difficult for them to settle in Germany; they migrate from community to community, mostly from one large town to another.

— But even those of the DP's who have money on the whole found it difficult to become part of the German-Jewish communities. In conversation, they are frequently very aggressive, even at social gatherings they often unexpectedly start to talk about their experiences in the concentration camps. Many of them still have the intention of emigrating.

— ... the difficulties encountered by about a third of the Jews who are living in Germany today: an insufficient command of the language and a lack of understanding of the German mentality.

— ... the deep contrast between the Jews from Eastern Europe and the native German Jews who have survived the camps or returned from exile. Again and again, the majority of those who were born in the country in some way or another found the East European Jews unacceptable socially and rejected their religious customs, and sometimes gave as a reason for their lack of participation in communal life their aversion to having anything to do with the East European Jews.

— The Jews from Eastern Europe and the Jews from Western Europe will have to overcome once and for all their opposition to each other. We should try to ignore the differences in background, customs and manners. We should try to concentrate on the similarity of our problems, and make allowances for habits acquired in a different society through a different upbringing. On one thing at least we ought to be agreed: we are all of us Jews, we have all of us been equally persecuted because we are Jews, we have all shared the same difficulties and are confronted today with the same task of making a new start in life.

— We will fight whatever might tend to separate us once again into two camps. Have we not all of us suffered as Jews?

— Are we not united by a common fate?

✡ *There must be unity amongst the Jews, there are no Polish Jews or German Jews, there are only Jewish Jews, a Jew is a Jew. (Ben Gurion)*

— We cannot and we shall not permit differences to be made between us today; no one shall be allowed to make a museum piece out of a German Jew as opposed to a Jew from Poland or anywhere else.

— It is inconceivable that a Jewish community (in Germany!) shall today treat a new member on admission according to his origin and nationality. It is an old tradition that every Jewish newcomer has the right automatically to become a member of the Jewish community of the district in which he settles.

— Many of those who are West European Jews today were yesterday Jews from Eastern Europe, and the East European Jews of today will be the future Jews of the West. This is the course of history, and certainly not a value judgement.

— The whole difference between old-established Jews and newcomers amounts to no more than that the first have settled here one or two generations earlier.

VII

THE INHERITORS

— Is there a future for Jews in Germany? We have not
forgotten the resolutions passed by various Jewish corporations
and organisations which proclaimed that no Jew should ever
again step on to German soil; indeed, there was even talk of a
cherem, a proscription and a curse, which would apply not only
to Germany but to every Jew who might be tempted to settle
there. It is an understandable reaction on the part of the Jewish
people . . . It smells of corpses here, of torture chambers and
crematoria. But there are in fact a few hundred thousand Jews
living in Germany today; the chaotic postwar years have even
turned a part of Germany into a collection centre for Jews.

— After the liberation, the predominant thought at the first
meeting of the leaders of the Berlin Jewish community was
that we ourselves should liquidate what life the final solution of
the Nazis had left in our community, and that we should arrange
the emigration of the survivors, especially to Eretz Israel and
America, as quickly as possible. And so, in the first few years
after the war, the Berlin community was always considered to be
in the process of liquidation. But over the years, the emigration
of those who had returned in addition to that of those who were
left proved to be very difficult to manage, due partly to the
political conditions in Palestine before the State of Israel came
into existence, partly to the red tape in obtaining the numerous
forms and affidavits necessary for immigrating into the American
countries. And then there was the influx of Jewish refugees from
the devastated regions of Eastern Europe . . .

— Of course we do not have here in Germany the peace and
quiet, the security, the leisure and the confidence in the future,
which are the most essential prerequisites for any cultural programme. All our activities have to be arranged according to the

philosophy of 'as if'. We have to work as thoroughly as if our programme for education were going to be needed for a long time to come, while we have to remain aware of the fact that all the arrangements which we are making will only be temporary and will not exist for long.

— The Jews in Germany have no reason to feel confident about the future. Only recently we have had evidence that sometimes and in some places there is no desire to make any changes at all; not only are our problems and difficulties insufficiently understood, but over and above that the attitude towards us is frequently plainly hostile. If this were really nothing more than a lack of understanding we would not consider it so alarming, because we could do something about it . . .

— In my opinion Germany no longer deserves to have any Jews. It has already shown once that it will not put up with us, and there are still signs—and that is the most disconcerting thing about the whole matter—that it wants to be rid of us. Sooner or later we will have to face the fact that it will be our task to dissolve the Jewish communities. Emigration will be the only solution for all those who are neither too sick nor too old.

— . . . that we are really intended to feel at home here. Two years after the war, there is unfortunately very little evidence that this is so, and we have neither the energy nor the time to wait much longer. That is why many, and by no means the worst of us, prefer an uncertain future in a foreign country; it is because we can't be sure of Germany that many of us decide to emigrate and to make our homes somewhere else.

— It is not lack of love for our native land which causes many of us to endeavour to leave this country; it is plain necessity which forces us out of Germany, because a large part of the population continues to regard us as inferiors, as outcasts. After we returned from the concentration camps, we played our part in Germany's reconstruction, with all our resources and to the best of our abilities. But we have to admit that the majority of Germans continue to regard us and our problems with the same indifference, and sometimes even with the same hostility, as years ago. In a way, therefore, for most Germans the Jewish question has never existed, and it does not exist for them today. We are fully aware that there are others who have stood up for us, who try very hard to understand us and to treat us fairly. But unfortunately, these are a small minority . . .

✡ *Of course it is perfectly understandable that a small proportion of the Jews tried to establish themselves temporarily here in Germany. But some of these optimists have already wound up their affairs or sold their assets at a loss and like the other Jews have left the country. Those who remain were forced by circumstances to come and wait here, because only here conditions were and are such that they will be given the opportunity of emigrating overseas and especially to Israel. There are not many Jews who dream of starting a new life in Germany or of settling here permanently. They were quickly enough obliged to realise that antisemitism was not yet dead but only asleep.*

— The Germans frequently say in so many words: 'What a pity that some of them have survived!' and as time passes anti-semitic incidents grow more frequent. The lack of understanding shown by officials, by the political parties and by the general population has made us alien outlaws in our native country, where we had hoped to spend the evening of our life in peace. Many of us would be very glad indeed to turn our backs on Germany for ever, but we are tired, physically and emotionally, and after all we have suffered we cannot face making a new start once more on alien soil, and anyway would not have the energy to do so successfully.

✡ *And it is a fact that of the Jews with whom I spoke those who intended to stay here invariably cited material reasons for their decision. Without exception, they too advocated emigration. They themselves were prevented from it only by purely personal considerations. Those of them who were already succeeding in earning a living were mostly afraid to burn their boats and venture destitute into an uncertain future. They have no relatives abroad, they can't speak the language, perhaps their professional qualifications would be useless elsewhere . . .*

— Even those who remained with the firm intention of emigrating gradually changed their minds, partly because they were managing to make a living, partly because they were tired of being refugees moving from place to place . . .

— Possibly, these people originally intended to emigrate. But for one reason or another they had never been able to make this wish come true. Some of them had to stay because either they themselves or a member of their immediate family was for reasons of health refused an entry visa into one of the receiving countries, some because they were no longer in a position to settle and earn a living elsewhere because of their advanced age; a third group resigned themselves to remaining here—they were simply too tired to continue for the rest of their lives as refugees. (Altogether there is much more apathy and despondency amongst the Jews in Germany than amongst any other group of people, because they have suffered such huge disappointments.)

— Most of us are old and sick people who have survived the time of the Nazis. These people are physically and emotionally so completely ruined, that they simply don't have the energy to rehabilitate themselves. Added to this, most of them simply lack the money which might have provided them with a reasonable standard of life.

— Many people have no one abroad waiting for them, to whom they could go, and are not in a position to re-establish themselves by their own efforts in a foreign country. Some of us here still have close ties with the Germans and don't feel that they could bear to sever these ties and get used to other surroundings. Some Jews have returned from abroad because they had never managed to settle down, and others have made a new start and re-established themselves. All these will remain in Germany . . . They are nevertheless good Jews . . .

✡ *The German Jews who stay do not feel young enough to start a new existence abroad, and they do not want to become a burden to others. But they all agree in their desire not to let their children remain in Germany, or to return there.*

— People ask us: 'Why are you still here? All the decent Jews have left long ago!' People refuse to allow for the fact that Jews are still living here either for health reasons or because they have difficulties concerning their emigration.

✡ *Between 1945 and 1952 more than 7,000 German Jews left for overseas, principally for the new State of Israel and the United States, which had eased its immigration laws.*

— In 1948, when we had our first opportunity to carry out a census and to question the Jewish population both in the towns and in the DP-camps, we were already forced to realise that between 18,000 and 20,000 Jews would find it difficult if not impossible to emigrate. They were sick, they were old, they had been left without one single relation anywhere, and our communities had to accept responsibility for them.

✡ *The registration for emigrating to Israel came to an end on 15th February 1949.*

✡ *More than 100,000 Jews were helped to leave Germany and brought to Israel. Nevertheless, more than ten thousand remain in Germany, for which there is no justification, not from a Jewish, not from a Zionist, not from a human point of view. The Jewish Agency for Palestine and the citizens of the State of Israel feel that this remnant of the Jewish population is in danger of assimilating and of deteriorating both morally and as Jews. Therefore, the Jewish Agency in Israel has decided to bring the activities of its legation in Germany to a close on 31st December 1949.*

✡ *And so the Jews living in Germany today are confronted with a spiritual dilemma, with a burden almost of accusation and guilt. No one maintains that the State of Israel was established entirely for their benefit, nor is it claimed that the State of Israel is in a position to offer a home to every Jew in the world. But considering the ideology which underlies the creation of the State of Israel, the Jews in postwar Germany might have been expected to be the first to seek shelter there, instead of contradicting all it stands for by deciding to aim at an independent existence in just that country which only a few years before had attempted the final solution.*

— The chief indictment against the Jews in Germany is that two years after the foundation of the Jewish State they still have not emigrated to Israel. But why not pronounce anathema against the American Jews, too? Surely the Jews in Germany, who have passed through the seven gates of hell, have the right to wait until conditions for settling in Israel have improved a little?

— We are reproached with the high incidence of mixed marriages; we are told that we are not sufficiently observant, that we do not know enough about Judaism and that we are not sufficiently interested in it—people overlook that all these criticisms also apply to the Jews in every other European country.

— Perhaps the Jews should leave Germany. With the same logic they should leave every other country of the diaspora.

✡ *Thus the Jews who after the war remained in Germany or returned there were faced with a threefold conflict:*

1. The unhesitating assumption by the Jews of the world and all their organisations that they would seize the first available opportunity to leave this country which had brought such a tremendous catastrophe upon their people;

2. The moral claim which the State of Israel has upon all Jews to participate to the best of their abilities in establishing a new home willing to receive them all; and

3. The problem of living as a Jew in Germany and amongst the Germans without being either able or willing to call themselves 'German Jews'.

— We are aware of our responsibilities as Jews and consider it our duty to look after those who have decided to live out their lives in Germany as well as to care for the old and the sick. Therefore, it has made us very sad to learn that the Zionist organisations are prepared to treat the Jews who live in Germany as the pariahs amongst the Jews of the world. We are prepared to come to an understanding with anyone who does not wish us harm. But we are not prepared to allow ourselves to be treated as second-class Jews.

— It seems frivolous to us to demand an unconditional emigration without at the same time being able to guarantee reasonable living conditions for our people who are mostly old and no longer capable of working. We feel responsible for the people in our care and as long as there are any Jews left in Germany, our communities will continue to exist in order to help them, no matter how energetically others may set a deadline for their liquidation. We will resist making common cause with anyone for the sake of the sort of collective hatred of which we ourselves have been the victims so often throughout our history.

— But the force of economic circumstances is greater than that of political resolutions. People who for various reasons could not manage to make a living in the countries to which they had emigrated but thought that they might be able to do so in Germany, will at least make the attempt to gain some measure of economic security in spite of all the resolutions passed by Jewish organisations abroad. On the other hand, there are some Jews who will decide not to emigrate because of their age, because of circumstances, and in many cases because of the fact that their non-Jewish partners have always stood by them; these are all people who have had difficulties enough in their lives.

— When one examines the particulars of the Jews who are living in Germany today, it becomes obvious why there will never be a complete emigration. In Berlin, over half the Jewish community is related to Germans—this applies with minor variations also to most of the rest of West Germany.

— Amongst those who remained, practical considerations may often have played the decisive part. One may call the category of those who returned incorrigible idealists: they do not deserve to be boycotted and despised.

— In fact, a large number of Jews are still considering their emigration. But it is only natural that people, confronted with circumstances beyond their control, first learn to accept and then no longer wish to change them. Therefore, in time they will get used to the fact that they have remained in Germany, and no longer question it.

— The Jews living in Germany remember the crimes committed against their relatives and friends just as clearly as those who have left the country. But it is our belief that they can claim to have regained a healthy objectivity much more quickly, and from a political point of view their decision to stay has proved far from unwise. But unwise is the criticism which groups of Jews abroad have not yet ceased to level against the continuing existence of a Jewish community in Germany. This community

—no matter how small—has shown in the difficult years after the war and will continue to show in the future that it possesses dignity and viability and a justifiable existence; moreover, it regards itself as an indivisible part of the Jewish people.

— Some may find it difficult to understand that the German Jews have remained, after all their physical and emotional experiences of the last fifteen years. We are no starry-eyed idealists. Our actions shall prove that we also are good Jews; we do not question for one moment that we belong absolutely and entirely to the Jewish people and its centre, the new State of Israel, even though we will continue to live here.

✡   *At night when I remember Germany,*
     I lie awake and cannot go to sleep. (Heinrich Heine)
✡   *Even if I were exiled from German soil, I would still remain a*
German. (Walther Rathenau)
— Either we are Germans or we belong nowhere.
— With the end of the cause of my exile, my exile itself comes to an end.
†   *Blessed are the homesick for they shall return. (Novalis)*
— I would rather have died in a concentration camp than have suffocated in exile.
— Not that we have been unfaithful to Germany—it was Germany which has been unfaithful to us. The difficult decision to settle down again here is a strictly personal one.
— Whether or not to return is a question which everybody has to answer for himself.
✡   *This unrequited love for Germany is a tragic element in our*
past and, apparently, it is also part of contemporary history. Some
leave because every stone here reminds them of what happened, and
some return because this is where their roots are.
✡   *It has always been like that for the Jews in Germany, ever since*
they first began to settle there: they were exiled, but they returned to
the country which a few years before had exiled them, returned, to be
exiled again . . .
— It is inconceivable and can be explained only by the deep love a Jew feels for the country of his birth, that in spite of

terrible catastrophes they have always, at the first possible opportunity, returned home.

— Partly because they did not feel at home in their new
countries, partly because their love for Germany, their native
land, was greater than any hatred or prejudice which they may
have felt.

— If only those people were concerned who were living under
difficult conditions, as for instance the refugees in Shanghai . . .
But some apply for repatriation from countries in which the
poorest are better off than the majority of people here.

— Some of them returned because they had what amounted to
a sentimental love for Germany, and had never ceased to believe
in the country. They mostly came out of sheer idealism, because
materially they had long ago established themselves in exile.

— . . . several reasons. One is that the German language and
landscape are the only ones in which we feel at home.

— An old Münchener Jew ought to live and die in Munich.

— Cologne—the city where my family has lived and wor-
shipped and been buried for a hundred and fifty years, the city to
which I belong . . .

— They will find the people here strangers, but they are quite
simply homesick for the country where they were born, for the
familiar places of their childhood; and they repeat over and over
that they feel that they have a duty here, which they want to
fulfil to the best of their abilities. They have conserved their
energies and they want to use them to re-educate the German
people.

— I believe that it ill becomes a former refugee like myself to
be a pessimist and to refuse to face the present Germany. All one
can do is return, look round and set to work, so that what happened can never happen again. I have never said that we should
forget. But I am convinced that we can help to shape the next
generation.

— We have returned because we considered it our duty to
help those of our fellow Jews who did not manage to emigrate.
But we also returned because we believed that the majority of
the Germans would support us . . .

— For us who have returned there was only one possibility: to return! But we have already been forced to realise that a large part of the German population has not changed at all, and that many old Nazis still occupy positions of power. But it is also true that a proportion—though a small one—does its utmost to attempt to make reparations for what has happened, and to begin to build a new, democratic Germany.

— ... because they were homesick for a Germany without Nazis, because they mistakenly believed that the defeat would bring the Germans to their senses, because they expected them spontaneously to express their regret for what has happened, and because they assumed that they would show a genuine willingness to make reparations. But after our experiences since 1945 ...

— ... back to Germany, where they will find many difficulties, many disappointments, and very few friends.

— Not much has changed, you wishful thinkers, homesick for your Germany of long ago ... Dear returning exiles, you will be very unhappy and very lonely, you will have to admit to your sorrow that you have returned a generation too soon—no, two generations!

— Who would have the courage to encourage them to take the risk of starting up the old process all over again? It would be excellent if the Germans could learn to overcome their anti-semitic superstitions. But in order to give them the opportunity to do this, do we have to be so reckless as to provide history with the chance of repeating itself?

— Whoever believes that Germany's defeat drove out race-hatred and the spirit of the Nazis is very much mistaken. Anyone who mixes with the people and listens to the conversations which are meant for their ears alone, will be amazed. Many of them feel that they are the innocent victims of a misfortune which they did not want to happen and have done nothing to bring about; and in the fact that they are Germans they recognise no responsibility at all. In their opinion, the few surviving Jews are still pushing to the head of the queue, demanding preferential treatment, as victims of fascism, to which they are not entitled, and are once more enslaving the poor German people by means of the many official positions which they occupy. Whoever returns must be prepared to reap a late harvest of hatred, not merely for himself but also for his descendants. The total picture is not encouraging for those who return. They will be unable to trust the people around them, who will invariably assure them that they considered Nazism a plague right from the start, and only joined the party—if at all—because otherwise they would have lost their jobs. Every one of them has his own Jew, whom he claims to have saved by having done this and that for him.

The total defeat, the desolate ruins of homes and other buildings, the dismantling of numerous factories, the collapse of the entire economy and all civil affairs and above all the depression belonging to a postwar period, all combine to a ghastly dissonance, heightened by the shortages of food, fuel, electricity and the most basic commodities. The people are like ravening wolves fighting over scraps, and everything done by the occupying powers to improve matters is only a drop in the ocean.

— Come back, come back—but without illusions!

† *We appeal to every refugee to return, we rejoice over every refugee who is prepared to return, and we will welcome him with open arms.*

— In his New Year's message, the mayor of Frankfurt expressed the hope that every former Jewish citizen would return. He promised them a warm and hearty welcome by the inhabitants of the town, and assured them that he would do everything in his power to make them feel at home again.

— Of course the Germans or rather, those who head the government, the municipalities, etc., are delighted by the appearance of spokesmen for 'German Jewry', as a sign that Germany's past sins are definitely forgiven, and as a confirmation of their hopes that the day is drawing near on which the world and the Jews will forget the mass exterminations. The authorities in Germany as well as their consulates abroad are very helpful to any Jew who wants to return to Germany. Of course it goes without saying that the majority of the Germans are against this policy. It has happened, that the reception which has met some Jews on their return to Germany has been no better than the treatment which once caused them to leave the country. The Jews in Germany today live in total isolation, alone and deserted, with an odd feeling, and though the atmosphere is not always hostile it certainly cannot be described as friendly.

✡ *Some Germans hoped for the return of the exiles because they thought that this would free them from their own burden of guilt. Often the welcome they extended to the Jews was no more than a callous attempt to say that bygones were bygones.*

— Dr. Schumacher has stated that Jews returning from exile should receive a hearty welcome. Considering that there are not enough apartments to meet the demand of the few thousand survivors, and that they are not given help enough to re-establish themselves, what hope is there for the Jews returning from exile? Shall these thousands of people after all they have been through come back merely to increase the misery here and to share our destitution?

— If their relatives here in Berlin were to describe to them the conditions truthfully, the shortage of food, the problem of housing, the difficulties of finding employment and the situation generally, not one of the refugees would wish for one moment to return to Germany.

— First of all, he would not find an apartment, and he would certainly not manage to get hold of any furniture. It is just possible that he would be able to resume his former occupation.

— In order to return, they would have to be as desperate as the Jews in Shanghai, who really did live for years under the most terrible conditions. We are afraid that even they will be disappointed when they return.

— Life in Shanghai is difficult for the Jews there. They are homesick for Germany and would very much like to return. They have no conception of the desperate situation of the Jews here in Berlin. In their imagination, Berlin still has the glamour of a bygone age. They have no idea of what things are really like.

We can't prevent anyone from returning home. We can only warn them against it.

— Two thousand five hundred German Jews, who are living

in Shanghai even today under the most ghastly conditions and who all of them want to return to participate in the reconstruction of Germany through helping to renew Jewish life there . . .

✡ *Except for these 'Shanghaiers', as other German Jews called them, no substantial or organised group of exiles returned to Germany after the war.*

— When I returned to Germany from Shanghai at the beginning of 1950, after having spent eleven years in exile, my first thoughts were probably those of everyone who returned: What are you going to do, how are you going to get on with the people around you? Are you going to be able to live with them?

It was clear to me that this was not really a return, that one was rather a newcomer. Friends and acquaintances from the years of exile, who had returned to Germany already a few years earlier, welcomed me and on the strength of their own experiences were the first to give me advice. They told me that when they had arrived in 1947 they had been greeted most warmly both by officials and by the population, who were glad to have at least a few of their former Jewish citizens back at 'home', and they were assured that everything would be done to make their existence as easy as possible. They were soon to find out that these were no mere empty words. They were helped with accommodation, they were helped with finding work—they were helped as much as possible.

By the time I returned—1950—this change of heart amongst the Germans was already no longer quite so noticeable. There were no reception committees and nobody offered to help me in any way. The atmosphere was already noticeably cool. And even when I arrived anywhere with a letter of introduction I was often told: 'If only you had come back two years ago!'

All this made me realise that I could not rely on anyone and had to manage for myself . . .

Although Jewish communities had been re-established wherever there were any Jews, there was very little contact among the members. I had the impression that although a Jewish community was felt to be necessary, the urge to live as a Jew, which used to be the common bond, no longer existed.

— I have returned—and I am very sad,
  and nothing is as it once used to be!
  I have not now the innocence I had
  before I witnessed the world's misery. (Gerty Spies)

VIII

REPARATIONS

† *The Federal Government, together with the majority of the German people, is aware of the infinite suffering brought upon the Jews in Germany and in the occupied territories under the reign of National Socialism. The German people has an obligation to make reparations, both morally and materially, for the unspeakable crimes committed in its name ... In conjunction with the representatives of Jewry and the State of Israel ... the Federal Government is prepared to work out a solution to the problem of material reparations, in order to prepare the way for coming to terms emotionally with this immense suffering. (Federal Chancellor Dr. Adenauer)*

— History demanded of the Federal Government that it should acknowledge this obligation.

— ... a debt of honour owed by the German people.

† *It may be argued that this declaration is three years too late and that it is in any case a mockery to talk of financial compensation for six million dead. For the sake of the German people, however, if not for the Jews, it is important that this declaration should be made; and the most practical proof of repentance is to compensate the survivors of that historic crime. (The Times, 4/10/1951)*

† *This persecution is without a precedent in history—and so is this making of reparations.*

✡ *... this childish expression, with its note of appeal to the compassion of those to whom it was addressed, seemed to be the only one suitable to describe the desire to do the impossible ... to provide for the dependants, to compensate the survivors for their physical sufferings and for the destruction of their lives, to reach a propitiatory agreement with Israel. In the midst of the ten thousand words of its declaration, the Federal Republic referred to it with two words, calling it: die Wiedergutmachung.*

— In 1945, when we returned from the camps and from forced

4

labour or came out of hiding, we were fired by the firm intention to work together with all the positive forces in Germany to turn the country into a democracy. At that time we were prepared to forgive the past, because we assumed that the Germans themselves were ready to make reparations for their crimes . . . The years between have been one long chain of disappointments . . . If such a declaration had been made long ago—how much suffering and how many bitter thoughts we would have been spared! We have no reason whatever to be overjoyed at this declaration—it was bound to be made.

This declaration will not be of much value unless the desire expressed in it is shared by the whole German people. If this is the case, it opens the way to a true reconciliation.

† *Legally, compensation may take two forms—restitution of property taken from the Jews by the Nazis and reparations for loss of life, imprisonment, dismissal from State employment, and loss of income. Restitution, which was ordered by the occupying powers in each zone, has been in progress for some time though it has proceeded slowly and against increasing opposition. There are many genuine difficulties—for instance, the present occupier of a Jewish house may have bought it quite innocently from a former Nazi—but too often the courts appear reluctant to enforce the law. Reparations, except for those entitled to receive five marks for each day they spent in a concentration camp, has hardly begun. Even now it is uncertain how far the government is prepared to go. Though Germany's ability to pay is at present limited, the important point is that the obligation should be recognised for the future and that these promises should be fulfilled in practice.*

— The purpose of this legislation must be to give our people that to which they are entitled.

— The payment of reparations does not mean that we will be receiving public assistance, but that our legal claims will be met and that we will be compensated for the damage which was done to us.

— The payment of reparations will make good some of the disadvantages from which we suffer today; it will put us on an equal footing with the rest of the population.

— When we consider the principle underlying the question of the payment of reparations we must bear in mind the fact that the position of the former German Jews has been irrevocably damaged, and that any attempt to compensate them, though it will make things easier for them, will not be able to undo the damage.

— The reparation payments for the crimes committed by the Nazis are intended to redress the balance. Therefore, they are not a present from the State, they are not privileges accorded to this or that group, and therefore they are also not public assistance grants. This legislation concerns legal claims. It settles the question of payment for damages for illegal and highly immoral acts. These include looting, confiscation of property, the abuse of the State's power and robbery and murder.

— To return to us what is ours, to compensate us for the damages, to atone for the crimes . . .

— The reparation payments set the pace for a return to normal life.

— . . .that reparations are not paid only by Christians to Jews. On the one hand, the group of claimants is not restricted to Jews, but includes anyone who has been persecuted for their religion, nationality, political opinions or resistance to the Nazis; on the other hand, the group of those liable to make payments includes not only Germans but American citizens and even Jews themselves.

— If all goes well with this legislation, it still will never amount to anything for the Germans to be proud of. It will remain a piecemeal gesture, vaguely expressing rather brave principles. Much more clearly discernable in it are certain traits of the German national character. But without these traits —or the efforts to overcome them—even less and certainly nothing effective would have been done.

✡ *More than one million children were killed because they were Jewish children; they could not be brought back to life by any legislation. But many survivors received pensions. Others received back part of their property. According to a fixed scale, most were compensated for their lost possessions, for loss of life, for the years of imprisonment, for damage to their health.*

— . . . that in the sense of making amends the reparation

payments will always be insufficient. No state and no government is in the position to pay compensation for the immense suffering, the physical damage, and the loss of life.

— No one can compensate us for our dead relations. And they are not trying to do so. But it has been realised in Bonn that the survivors must be given back everything of which they have been deprived, and that in addition their lives must be made a little easier.

— And all the efforts which are now being made to make amends can never begin to hope to be adequate, because it is simply impossible to redress the sort of thing that happened during the persecution by means of civil legislation and the usual procedures.

— No one can compensate us for our sacrifices—for the loss of our husbands and our wives, our parents and children, our brothers and sisters.

— No attempt to make reparations can ever hope to suffice. The dead cannot be brought back to life, the survivors will never escape the consequences of their persecution.

— At most one could call it making atonement.

— None of us ever thought that making reparations was a financial problem, that is, that it was primarily a question of material compensation.

Any bargaining which takes place deprives the reparation payments of all moral and political value. To point out to the concentration camp survivors what has already been done for them since 1945, and to draw comparisons between them and the German refugees from the East, betrays such an utter lack of appreciation of what this is all about, that there is no point in discussing it any further.

If those Germans who really have their country's interest at heart do not feel sufficiently compelled by common decency to make reparations—as far as this is possible—for ethical reasons, purely practical considerations ought to convince them to do so. Sooner or later it must be in Germany's own best interest to enter into proper diplomatic and commercial relations with the State of Israel.

✡ *If Germany is to recover, it needs the good will of the world.
To obtain foreign aid, to be allowed to rearm, to become a partner
to the treaties amongst the free nations—all this depends upon the
world's moral approval. And the way to get the world's moral
approval is through large and small payments demonstrating the
making of reparations to the Jews. One frequently wonders : are the
politicians of postwar Germany sincerely decent-minded—or
practical? Perhaps a bit of both.*

— The future of the Germans depends upon their courage to
attempt to make reparations.

— It would after all be to Germany's own advantage to continue the legal rather than the illegal traditions of the state.

† *More than material considerations are involved in the making
of reparations. Morally and politically it is a necessity.*

— Germany's attitude over the reparation payments to the
victims of political, racial and religious persecution has become a
symbol of its humanity, a question of a people's political
maturity.

— It is in the interest of Germany's domestic economy that
those who have legal claims shall not be a charge on public assistance. It is in the interest of Germany's domestic as well as of its
foreign policy, that immediate and satisfactory arrangements
should be made to compensate the Jewish victims of National
Socialism and to help them to re-establish themselves in life.

— Not only justice but the immediate interests of the Federal
Republic demand that the Jewish communities and their institutions should be able to meet their financial commitments.

— It must be remembered that as a result of Hitler's final solution not many Jews have survived to claim reparations.

— Many who were the victims of the Nazis have now become
the victims of the lapse of time between the thought of making
reparations and the deed.

— Anyone who would care to take the trouble to work out how
much money has been saved by the death of Hitler's victims
since the end of the war would arrive at quite a large sum.

— Contrary to the 'astronomical' figures reported in the press,
the amounts actually involved are only a fraction of what the

Jews were once made to pay without any public outcry. Unless
we can find a decent solution to the problem of making moral
amends as well as of paying reparations, Germany will for ever
be excluded from the ranks of the civilised nations.

† *Justice cannot ask: 'how much?'*

† *... that the reparation payments are not a question of doing
sums but of fulfilling a moral obligation.*

† *This is a historic undertaking, which cannot be treated like an
ordinary financial transaction.*

† *It is the duty of every German to compensate the Jews for what
we have done to them, so that he may free his conscience from the
burden which each of us must carry. (Kurt Schumacher)*

— The Germans are watching their debt mount. It is not our
fault that it is so huge.

† *Whether or not the Federal Government is economically in a
position to pay reparations is a question which must not even be
asked. The Germans under Hitler did not ask the Jews whether
they could manage to bear their sufferings.*

— If 60 million Germans are not able to meet the basic needs
of the 20,000 survivors, one must assume that the obstacle is not
lack of means but lack of intention, then one must look in vain
for the change of heart which ought to precede the reparation payments ...

† *We must achieve peace with Israel at no matter what cost.
(Erich Lueth)*

— This question concerning money must be answered with
moral considerations.

— The Bible speaks of the rending of garments and adds that
people ought rather to rend their hearts. The Germans have
recently been rending their garments; let us hope that this
symbolises a change of heart.

— Money and bricks are the most tractable means with which
to make reparations.

— To pay compensation and return what belongs to us is not
enough; to make reparations which will be of some moral value
demands something more.

— The payments by themselves do not make reparations; they

ought at least at the same time to have the effect of making the spirit of National Socialism morally and politically unacceptable.

— Just as the Germans could not have discharged their moral obligations to the Jews by a change of heart alone, so to limit the idea of reparations to the payment of money is also morally untenable.

— The solution of the financial problems has nothing to do with the historic question of a reconciliation between our two peoples.

— If the problem of making reparations cannot be solved completely, it will not have be solved at all.

† *We owe the Jews far more than reparation payments. How can we pay this other debt if they are no longer willing to live among us? If we should finally fail to experience a change of mind and a change of heart, our people will be left with a pernicious trauma.*

— We expect them to realise that they were wrong. The most important thing is that they should change their attitude. We ask no more and no less of the Germans than a change of heart and of mind.

IX

THE NEW COMMUNITIES

✡ *And they that shall be of thee shall build the old waste places: thou shalt raise up the foundations of many generations. (Isaiah 58,12)*

— We who have survived must ask ourselves today, ten years after the war: Have we shown ourselves worthy of having been saved?

— Will any Jewish community in Germany be able to forget that only a few years ago Jewish citizens were outlawed, made to wear a yellow star, exiled, despoiled, excluded from professional and social life and finally exterminated? How can our presence here be reconciled with human dignity and an awareness of our people's history?

✡ *Things are not easy for these Jews. They live at a time and in a place showing every sign of change; they cannot be sure of the ideology or the politics of their surroundings.*

— We have received nothing for which we did not first have to ask and to go on asking. We have had to fight for whatever we have achieved, and sometimes we ask ourselves, with the most serious misgivings and the gravest doubts, if what we have achieved really amounts to anything much.

— And so it had to be small achievements which marked the beginning of the reconstruction. These small achievements are the milestones indicating the gradual consolidation of the new Jewish communities in Germany.

— New life—in a small way—has arisen out of chaos and ruin.

✡ *The small group of survivors could hardly claim to be the successors of German Jewry; they would have found it difficult to continue its important and distinguished tradition. There were amongst those who remained almost no teachers or cantors, much less any people of distinction who might have come forward as the spiritual leaders. This small number of survivors was scattered over the whole of West Germany. The new communities did not even include all of this group; they were joined by only between 6–8,000 of those who might have become members. The high death-rate amongst these predominantly old people has since reduced the figure by about 3,000.*

✡ *. . . died as a result of the effects of their persecution on their health and on their will to live. The German-Jewish mortality rate, twice that of the general German population . . .*

— There are fewer and fewer survivors, because the death-rate amongst the former victims of the persecution is so appallingly high.

✡ *The survivors from the concentration camps die young.*

— With few exceptions, after the mass emigration the remaining Jewish communities are very small indeed. The overwhelming majority of their members are people who have for some reason or other so far found it impossible to emigrate. These small and very small communities lead a miserable, isolated, sorrowful existence; almost no one cares what becomes of them.

— After those who were able to emigrate—mostly younger people—have left, the number of Jews remaining in Germany may be estimated at about 25,000; of these, a considerable proportion is in need of financial assistance and in even greater need of advice and moral support. They are on the average 55 years old.

— We are a community of old people only.

— Eighteen of the communities have more members over 70 than under 20 years old; in addition to lacking the age-structure of a normal population, many of the communities also lack the normal balance between the sexes—these facts combined create a very odd impression.

— The Jewish community in Germany continues to bear witness to the past catastrophe. Its 25,000 members live scattered over 70 communities. In Berlin, Jewish life has revived more than elsewhere. There are here about 4,000 Jews who have already re-established many institutions: a hospital, an old people's home, a women's guild, a students' union. Slowly, very

4*

slowly, Jewish life revives. 45 per cent of the members of our
community are in need of financial assistance.

— Since 1950, more people have been returning from exile
than have emigrated, and although emigration continues, and
although there is an exceedingly high death-rate, the membership of the Jewish communities in Germany has slowly grown.

— About 6,000 former DP's have joined the communities (it
is estimated that a further 2,000 to 4,000 are living in Germany
unidentified as Jews).

— This new membership meant that our community included
again, for the first time since the war, young married couples
and their children, who had been born since 1945. Until then we
had had almost no younger members and no children.

— The majority of the people who make up the Frankfurt
community, for instance, lived formerly in other districts or
outside Germany; so that the origin of our members today, their
way of life, their ideas and attitudes, are much more various than
they used to be. There has not been time enough since 1945 to
blend all these so very dissimilar elements into one organic
whole.

— ... the Munich community, made up of 95 per cent former
DP's, Poles, Lithuanians, Hungarians, etc., and only five per
cent former German citizens of Jewish faith (altogether 3,181).

— In Munich, Frankfurt-on-Main and many other towns
of the former American zone of occupation, the great majority of
the members of the Jewish communities are former DP's, whose
presence has played a decisive part in the revival of Jewish life
there. Most of the Jews who come from Eastern Europe have
much closer ties with Jewish national and religious traditions and
customs than the surviving German Jews, who mostly escaped
the persecution only because they were married to Gentiles who
were able to prevent their deportation.

— One really ought not to call the Jews who are living in
Germany today 'German Jews'—as we were once able to call
ourselves with pride. Only some of us have known the country in
the good old days.

— At least a third of the Jews who are living in Germany

today grew up in Eastern Europe and have difficulties in learning the language and in understanding the mentality of the people. In addition, these are people who were mostly adolescents at the time of the persecution; they have never received any formal education or training and in most cases they are the only survivors of their families. In every respect they have been uprooted; above all they are unused to regular work.

— Most members of our community are people who have come to Germany by chance and who by chance were left stranded here after the general exodus. A large number of these people . . . have suffered much and are in need of financial and social assistance if they are not to perish in poverty and want. For years they have been living temporary lives, either they could not manage their affairs because they were ill, or they just let things slide. Public relief is no longer so easily available, and anyway can do no more than save them from starvation. It does not prevent their more and more rapid descent into utter destitution. For these people, the housing problem becomes more urgent, the question of finding work is never settled and, in addition, the general atmosphere is hostile to Jews.

— . . . that for most of the Jews life has become hopeless, sad and miserable. The welfare centres are overwhelmed by requests, and have not the means to satisfy a fraction of the needs. In the first few years after the war, the international relief organisations were very generous and helped us tremendously. Today we can no longer count on them because their obligations lie somewhere else.

It is very sad that so many people, who were once living in easy circumstances, are now dependent upon charity.

— It is really a pity about the Jewish statistics. Ten years after the war more recipients than contributors, more homeless than homes, more sick than healthy.

— The housing conditions are predominantly bad, the state of health almost always unsatisfactory. The concentration camps have left their ineradicable traces and the majority of these survivors suffer from recurrent outbreaks of chronic illness.

— The welfare office of the Berlin Jewish community provides assistance for about 800 people, that is roughly 20 per cent of the town's Jewish population. This relatively high figure is to be explained partly by the age structure of the Berlin Jewish community, partly by the number of exiles returning to Berlin (between 40 and 50 persons each month). The municipality's rate of assistance is insufficient to provide an adequate minimum for people who have suffered twelve years of persecution.

— Alone they returned from the concentration camps and alone they have remained. Each of them carries about within him the slow poison of some illness, the depression of his isolation, the wilderness of exile, and a hopeless passion for life. Thus endowed, what prospects do people have?

— Our people are physically and emotionally exhausted, socially and economically more or less ruined, and the equality which we have regained before the law does not automatically cancel these disadvantages. And so it is to be expected that so far only a few of us have succeeded in re-establishing ourselves in general life at a level approaching our former positions.

— The overwhelming majority of the Jews are finding it difficult to make a living. For older people it is almost impossible to hold their own against German competition. Only very few Jews, certainly not more than one per cent, have succeeded in establishing themselves as independent businessmen; they were the only ones who had the necessary capital. Many Jews manage to eke out a living as small shopkeepers who are of no importance. Nobody need therefore be surprised that some Jews become publicans, or pedlars trading without a fixed place of business. Apart from the few hundred officials and secretaries of the Jewish communities, very few Jews are working as employees. Few of the workmen are sufficiently skilled in their trade to make a good living. Between 15 and 20 per cent of the Jews are managing on their pensions and about 30 per cent are living on public assistance. There is also a whole group of people who have no means and no income at all; these are mostly exiles who have returned and do not qualify for assistance. It is a dismal picture which does not augur well for the future.

— Neither the few Jewish businessmen who have re-established themselves since 1945 nor the many people receiving public assistance can be considered as truly representative of the general Jewish population living in Germany today. This consists mainly of skilled and unskilled workmen and people trading in a small or a very small way. There are almost no manufacturers. By comparison with former times, there are very few Jewish lawyers, doctors, artists and other professional people. An obvious indication of this is the still almost completely undeveloped Jewish cultural life.

— Of the many Jewish doctors who left Germany, very few returned. There are probably no more than 35 of them in all, about 25 of whom are living in West Berlin. It was relatively easy for doctors to pass the additional examination required of them before they were allowed to practise in the countries in which they had made their homes; the situation of the judges and lawyers was considerably more difficult. Today there are in the Federal Republic more than 400 lawyers, of whom between 50 and 60 have been appointed judges, some with very high rank. Three Jews have been elected to the new Federal Diet. The first postwar West German Government already included Jews, who made their contribution to the development of the Federal Republic.

— A relatively large proportion of surviving German Jews are married to Gentiles, which has had the effect of making the social rather than the religious life of primary importance within the Jewish communities in Germany today.

— The leaders of the communities are usually Jewish men married to Gentile women, as most of the survivors in fact belong to this group. These people, drawn by the force of circumstances to the centre of communal affairs, had rarely played any part in them before Hitler came to power.

— Those who belonged to the remnant of German Jewry now felt themselves to be members of the Jewish community because they too had been persecuted as Jews.

✡ *The Jewishness of many of the survivors thus consisted only of their share in the hardships suffered under the Nazi regime.*

— ... because the traumatic experience of being persecuted as
a Jew makes a person into a Jew, it seems to me, regardless of his
religious or ideological beliefs.

— The leaders of the present-day Jewish communities—they
may be seen sociologically as an 'elite'—form so to speak the first
generation of 'Marranos'. As young people most of them may well
have thought and felt themselves to be Jews and observed some of
the Jewish traditions. The majority of their children did not
receive a Jewish upbringing, nevertheless they have remained
very definitely conscious of their Jewish parentage. They are
'Marranos' in that they are ignorant of the Judaism which they
have finally come to profess again, in that they want to acquire
knowledge and understanding of it, and also in that they remain
uncertain about identifying themselves with religious Judaism.

— Because these new Jews lack almost every kind of Jewish
tradition, they may quite possibly fail in their attempt to return
to Judaism and its spiritual sources.

— They were in doubt on almost every question of religion,
and almost every one of their decisions was arbitrary.

— Religious difficulties arose not only out of the structure of
the communities, but also out of the fact that they were visited
by a great many different rabbis. Coming from America, England
and Australia, most of them stayed in Germany for only a short
time. They varied from the strictly orthodox to the liberal or
reform. Whose teaching was the Jewish community to follow?

— The problem of the spiritual care of the slowly developing
community is raised already in the minutes of the first committee meetings, and it continues to be raised throughout the years.

— Many of the DP's from Eastern Europe were steeped in
Jewish learning and only wanted to be convinced ('Where was
God?'); the German survivors knew almost nothing about
Judaism. What was suitable for some members of the community
was not always suitable for all of them.

— Only a small proportion of the Jews who are living in Berlin
today have been brought up within some sort of Jewish tradition.
Nevertheless, the members of our community have a strong
sense of belonging, and they want to return to Judaism. The

differences between the various Jewish tendencies are gradually losing their importance. The orthodox Jews have been obliged to relinquish some of their old customs; on the other hand, many non-practising Jews have begun to keep some of the observances. It used to be the conservatives versus the liberals and the Zionists versus the non-Zionists, today we do not oppose each other any more. If only we had at least one rabbi in Berlin, we would be able to overcome all our religious difficulties.

— Before the Nazis came to power we were liberal or orthodox, we were advocates of Zionism or of assimilation. Now we must put our differences aside, because first of all we have to re-establish our community.

— Immediately after the war there was a great deal of Jewish religious and cultural activity in Germany. Numerous organisations, officials and parties were extremely interested and supported every Jewish community as much as possible by sending them teachers and speakers and by arranging lectures and courses. Every community was alive with every kind of Jewish activity. People talked Hebrew; there was a particular interest in Hebrew courses and in religious instruction. Neither time nor money was spared to meet our cultural needs and to raise the general level of education. Numerous Hebrew schools were established, Jewish sports-clubs were founded, Jewish groups provided every kind of entertainment; a great many visitors from Israel, from the United States, from France, brought news and information from the Jews of the world into our communities.

And what are things like today?

— During the first few years after the liberation tremendous efforts were made, especially by the Jews in Israel and the United States, but also by Jews elsewhere, to provide for us a Jewish cultural life and above all to bring us closer to secular and religious Judaism. But after the majority of the DP's had emigrated and their camps had been closed, though some Jews still remained, most of this cultural activity came to an end. For instance, here in Munich we used to have a very good Hebrew high school. All over Germany there were theatrical companies. We were able to see Jewish films. There were many libraries with a good selection of Hebrew and other Jewish books, and we were provided with a large choice of newspapers and periodicals written by and for Jews. All this belongs to the past.

— In most towns almost nothing is being done in the cultural field. Cultural events are rare indeed. Most of the organisations have ceased to exist and those that remain have almost ceased to function. On rare occasions we are able to see a Jewish film; there are very few lectures, and practically no conferences. We are left with the impression that people no longer care what becomes of us.

— ... so that people who are living in the smaller communities feel lost and deserted and have no reason to hope that things will improve for them.

— There are a great many places in which the few Jewish residents are completely cut off from Jewish religious and cultural life and left to their own devices.

— All our problems are made much more difficult by the dispersion of the Jews in Germany into tiny groups living in utter isolation—a dispersion within the dispersion. Not only is there a great shortage of rabbis, but there are also almost no young assistants, almost no Jewish teachers, almost no cantors, the community is managed by mostly unqualified personnel and the rabbis are overwhelmed with social problems ...

— We have at the present moment almost no outstanding people to whom we could look for guidance and whose importance and standing in our community would make them our spokesmen.

— ... almost no teachers or scholars of distinction who are still active in their field.

— Unfortunately, there is in our small community no one who has anything to offer us. In the first few years after the war, we were at least occasionally invited to events taking place in the nearest larger community. That is something we miss very much. The leaders of our organisations are at least able to attend a Leo-Baeck-evening, a Maimonides-celebration. Nothing like that is offered to the rest of us.

Why are there no Jewish books or pamphlets published in Germany? It ought not to be impossible to provide us with translations of the works of Hebrew or English writers. There is money enough for other things . . .

There are the holidays—why does no one arrange for the young people from the various districts to meet each other; why do we not have a conference now and again?

When are we going to get some teachers?

Why do we not have more rabbis?

— Jewish community life in Germany is barren, it lacks heart . . . Even those who have returned to their old environment feel isolated and keep within their own small circle.

— Precisely because people are miserable and isolated this is the time to encourage and organise cultural activities. This applies not only to the Jewish education of our few children and adolescents but perhaps even more to the spreading of Jewish knowledge amongst the adults.

— We have barely begun our cultural activities. Now some of the reparation money is to be made available by the Claims Conference to our communities for cultural purposes. Until now, the building of the many new synagogues, the very existence of our communities has depended upon these funds. In the whole of West Germany there are eight rabbis, most of whom travel from one community to another . . .

✡ *In 1954 German reparation money became available through the Claims Conference. The building programme initiated then has been of such intensity and magnitude and on such a scale that it is unprecedented in European Jewish life. The result has been the appearance of what has been called 'a new Jewish skyline' in Europe. Synagogues, community centres, schools, hospitals, homes for the aged, children's homes, have risen from the rubble that was postwar Europe. The revival and rebirth of European Jewish life have taken tangible shape in glass and concrete, in steel and stone as well as in the minds and bodies of those who survived the holocaust.*

— And so, new schools, new synagogues are being built with the indirect help of those who have left us for ever.

— The best thing that has happened in Frankfurt during the past year has been the building of the community centre, which will provide us with schoolrooms, clubrooms and a lecture hall.

The building is intended mainly for the young, but it will also serve the rest of the community as a meeting place. The building, which has cost a lot of money, has been financed by the county of Hessen, and the interior furnishings by donations from the municipality of Frankfurt, the county of Hessen and the 'Joint'
— The synagogues are being rebuilt, the cemeteries are renovated, nursery schools and old people's homes are established or modernised. Libraries are restocked, youth groups are organised, and there is even a programme for adult education. In short, an attempt is being made to develop an active modern community life by copying the trend of many American Jewish communities of providing a community centre with every amenity.
— That new synagogues are being built is symbolical of the eternal 'nevertheless' which should comfort not only Jews but every human being, because it looks beyond the events and uncertainties of the day towards the future.
— The first synagogues which arose to replace those which had been destroyed by the Nazis were so to speak symbolical of the vitality of the Jewish community, of its determination to reconstruct a promising existence. The first to rebuild their synagogues were the larger communities.
✡ *By building a synagogue we add something of our own to the place we live in—it indicates what the place means to us. (Leo Baeck)*
— Now that the synagogues are being rebuilt in Germany we are again completely at home.
— We would like to regard the rebuilding of this synagogue as proof that the history of German Jewry has after all not come to an end, that we are at least a postscript . . .
— A synagogue is the only thing which gives Jews in the diaspora a sense of security. When every small community in the Federal Republic is firmly established, we may hope that German Jewry as a whole will be able to survive.

ADDITIONS

— There used to be a hundred DP-camps; the last of them, Foehrenwald . . .

✡ . . . *often referred to by the name of the nearest village, Wolfratshausen, was comparable to an American low-rent housing project. It had been built for the workers of a nearby munition factory; the Alpine setting was in the best Bavarian tradition.*

— In fact, Foehrenwald is a small self-contained town of 295 houses built solidly of stone. In the centre is the 'market place', with a tall flagpole from which the Star of David flutters against the Bavarian sky. The Jews no longer look up at it hopefully.

— In 1952, when the emigration of the DP's was assumed to have come to an end and the I.R.O.* ceased its activities, there remained in Germany roughly 12,000 DP's of whom about 2,000 were living in Foehrenwald and refused to leave the camp. The DP question, which the East European Jews themselves had considered political, now became an apparently insoluble problem for the welfare authorities.

— A short time ago, Foehrenwald became the responsibility of the Germans; it contains about 2,000 DP's of whom more than a third are sick people. Amongst the most unfortunate are the 'post-TB-cases', for whom emigration is impossible. That also applies to their families. There are about 300 of these DP's who, although they are quite fit, are not eligible for emigration, and are condemned to remain in Germany, together with an equal number of their relations. These people are becoming desperate, they threaten a hunger strike. Israel is ready to receive them, but the climate there would be very bad for their health. The Americans consider them sick and therefore excluded by their

*International Refugee Organisation. The I.R.O. had the basic responsibility for feeding, clothing, providing medical care, and paying the cost of resettling the DP's.

immigration laws. Yet other officials exclude these same people from the care for the sick, and pronounce them sound. Of course, they are in fact healthy and capable of doing useful work . . .

— These people are no worse than the rest of us; but because they are a collection of people dependent upon the help of others there is a tendency to look at them through a magnifying glass. Understandably enough, they arouse suspicion. They do in fact still live in a sort of ghetto and their very existence reminds people of the past which everyone wants to forget. These survivors from the concentration camps are the ones who have suffered most, the worst TB cases and other unfortunates, whose lives are still in pieces because no one has given them the help to mend them.

— Camp children—after ruining their childhood, antisemitism has made them the buck of society, outcasts who don't belong anywhere. In conversation, they hear for the first time the word *Lumpenproletariat* (the scum of society). 'But that means us!' an intelligent boy exclaims. 'We exist on charity and donations!' The other children nod agreement; I am deeply moved because the realisation shocks them. Under normal circumstances, these boys and girls would still be going to school or they would be serving a proper apprenticeship to some trade. Nevertheless, astonishingly enough, precisely this age group (15–17) is not at all embittered. They don't hate the Germans, and of their own accord reach the conclusion that there are just as many 'decent' people in Germany as anywhere else.

It is different with the older age group (18–25): they have suffered even more and been more aware of it, and every wasted year diminishes their chances of achieving a better future. They have even become tainted by Nazi thinking. They talk a lot about 'German blood', and about race and inborn racial characteristics. 'All Germans are born with the desire to kill,' one of them repeats mechanically; without exception, every one of his relations has been gassed. He is vehemently contradicted. But the whole discussion is on a lower level than that of the younger group. The older girls take no part at all—the demoralising influence of camp life is much more noticeable.

They cannot manage to come to terms either with antisemitism or with their own problems—these hundred or more young people whose ages range from fifteen to twenty-five—as long as they have to live in Foehrenwald or any other camp. A sixteen-year-old girl said: 'Everyone in the camp is psychologically damaged. No one is quite normal.'

✡ *In the early 1950's, several thousand DP's left again the countries to which they had emigrated from Germany after the war, and settled in Germany. Approximately one thousand Jewish DP's without passports or visas returned from Israel. When they were apprehended in Germany they were sent to Foehrenwald.*

Most of them obtained transit visas to neighbouring countries, then crossed the German border. They're called 'exiles who have returned' but they are not German Jews. The only element of 'return' is that they may have started from a German camp when they originally left for Israel. Some were never in Germany at all. They are drawn here because more agencies and machinery for emigration are located in Germany than anywhere else in Europe. They've heard that wandering Jews can get cash support from the agencies and even from the German authorities.

— As soon as the government there allowed them to travel, they left Israel either because they could not earn a living there or because their health suffered under the climate.

Unlike the old-established inhabitants of Foehrenwald, these are chiefly younger people, roughly between the ages of 25 and 45. Most of them are willing to work and some of them have a good trade; amongst others there are mechanics, butchers, tailors . . . Most of them want to emigrate.

✡ *Those who returned 'illegally' from Israel received no assistance from any quarter, until finally the German police authorities granted them pedlars' licences.*

These exiles who had returned 'illegally' were soon joined by a steady trickle of legal ones who hoped to find business prospects better in Germany than in Israel. Competent observers estimated their number at 4,000, but there were probably more, since many registered as foreign visitors although they came with the intention of remaining.

— The Refugee Relief Act and other measures enabled the majority of these last inhabitants of Foehrenwald to emigrate; about 900 people were helped to settle in various neighbouring towns. The 'Joint' made them grants to furnish their homes and helped them to establish themselves in their trades and professions.

— ... granting sums of money including large amounts to cover their living expenses for the duration of one year, to each family emigrating to South America and other countries, and providing those who remain in Germany with grants to buy furniture and other household necessities. To those unable to emigrate the German authorities have promised their assistance in finding work and accommodation, and every support until they have established themselves. In addition, the 'Joint' is making financial provisions for the so-called hard-core cases in Foehrenwald—the old, the chronic sick, the physically handicapped—to be cared for in institutions. Thus many people who have spent almost ten years in DP-camps will be enabled to live again in dignity and security, and the fit among them will become self-supporting.

✡   *Homesick reparations-pensioners.*
German nationals marked 'imperfect'.
Super-assimilationists.

— The communities began to show German Jewish characteristics ... even when the returning exiles did not become the leading members.

— Mostly, the people concerned have had no personal experience of the persecution. People who have been in the camps almost never return.

— The people concerned mostly could not tolerate the climate of their new country, they were not strong enough to work under the prevailing conditions, or they were unable to find suitable work.

— Something all these returning exiles have in common—they are destitute, sick, or very old.

— They are familiar with conditions in Germany as they were

twenty years ago, and even if at that time they had established
positions, they will find things different today and very difficult.
At their age, they won't find it easy to get work. There is a grave
danger that the difficulties of making a new start will discourage
and defeat them.

— The first thing which has to be considered is that 20 to 25
years have passed since their emigration and that therefore the
exiles are returning to a strange country, returning often with
dread and many reservations. Socially and economically, Germany
has changed fundamentally; their old personal and business
connections no longer exist, and so the returning exiles frequently
find themselves up against an insuperable wall. These problems
will have to be faced not only by the old, but by younger people
as well. Under the circumstances, there is very little chance that
those who are over 60 years old will be able to re-establish themselves after their return.

— ... that the Jews who return after twenty years are too old
and no longer belong.

— Not only were the communities to which the exiles returned
much smaller, but their members were people who had already
overcome their worst problems and made the necessary adjust-
ments. Much tact and patience was needed to re-create slowly a
basis for mutual understanding.

— People who have returned to Germany after the war and
tried to take part in Jewish affairs are sometimes reproached, in
a moment of crisis, by other Jews who spent the decisive years
in the purgatory itself, that they lack the experience necessary to
understand the postwar Jew. A sensitive person who finds himself thus excluded will raise no objections, because he himself
has a bad conscience.

Certainly, he will not believe and no one will tell him that he
ought to have offered himself for extermination. Nevertheless,
it is a fact that, firstly, he did not share the basic experience of
our generation of Jews, and secondly, he spent the time in com-
parative safety ... Not that he has done anything to make him
guilty, nevertheless he is guilty ... Perhaps he has committed
an 'unintentional sin' in the Jewish meaning of the phrase ...

— For psychological reasons, the number of Israelis in Germany is usually exaggerated. We estimate that there can certainly be no more than 5,000 of them.

— In the German Federal Republic, those who receive reparation payments can manage to live on them. This partly explains why the exiles return; it should not be misinterpreted as a rejection of Israel.

— Some return for personal reasons—reasons of health, for instance a number of older German Jews, who have received reparation payments, have returned to live on their capital or their pensions in an easier climate; or their reasons were to rejoin other members of their families. Considering that any immigrants from Germany who wanted to leave Israel were unable to do so for fifteen or more years, it would not have been surprising if the reaction had been even greater.

† *Jews who were German citizens or residents and who either emigrated or were expelled or deported between 30th January 1933 and 8th May 1945, will receive an immediate grant of 6,000 DM. There is no obligation upon those receiving this grant to return to their former place of residence; they may settle anywhere within the German Federal Republic and West Berlin.*

— This immediate grant was made available in order to make it easier for exiles returning to re-establish themselves and ought therefore to be awarded to all who qualify for it without special investigations and without red tape. Those returning may also expect to receive every assistance from the authorities, especially from the housing authorities.

— Exiles who have returned or who are now returning will find it easier to settle with the help of this grant; but beyond its utility it serves the purpose of making them feel welcome.

✡ *A resettlement grant—providing they were former German citizens. The claims for reparation payments from people over sixty-five years of age were treated as urgent, and so the old tended to return rather quickly.*

— Twelve years after the war, the number of Jews returning from exile to Berlin has risen considerably within the last few months. Every month, about 60 former residents return, so that

the Berlin Jewish community will soon have reached a membership of 5,000. An overwhelming number of those who return are
old, sick, and destitute.

✡   *Once these elderly people were back home, they tended to retire
from active life and to join the vast and very German army of
'pensioners'.*

*They felt insecure on returning to a country in which they had
suffered as children and from which they had been expelled. Having
been mistreated as Jews in their youth, they assumed that they
encountered hostility because they were Jews, even when they were
unpopular only as individuals.*

— As soon as they have settled again in Germany, these Jews
are automatically exposed to a fresh process of assimilation,
which they can escape only at the cost of keeping entirely to
themselves ... out of the not altogether unreasonable fear of a
repetition of past events, out of an understandable hatred; out of
a feeling of being second-class Jews and because they don't
really belong to any of the various Jewish groups.

— When the exiles began to return, the communities became
not merely larger but also more important, and there arose
disagreements about the purpose which they were intended to
serve. Many of the exiles returned with young children for whose
Jewish education they expected the communities to be responsible.
The communities accepted this new obligation as a matter of
course and intensified their cultural activities. But there arose
in consequence the question of whether the Hebrew used should
follow the Ashkenazit pronunciation customary in the diaspora
or the Sephardit pronunciation used in everyday life in Israel;
this in turn demanded an examination of the attitude of the Jews
in the diaspora to the question of Zionism.

— The flood of returning exiles in the years 1955-59 is
explained by their average age. The majority of these people
want to retire. Most of the Jewish pensioners will offer as a
reason the fact that the disablement and old age pensions paid
by Germany are worth more in that country than they are
abroad. Exiles who are still young or no more than middle-aged
who return also do so mainly for economic reasons, and the part

played by the reparation payments is quite obvious. The majority of these exiles have returned not in order to make a new start, much rather, they are at this late stage in their lives trying, as far as possible, to repair the damage, to put right their personal fate. They had decided to return to a country which had almost no synagogues, no rabbis or teachers to give their children a Jewish education; there was even little chance that they would be able to obtain kosher provisions.

— Everyone who has returned knew what he was doing and that he cannot be sure of anything. But he has made his decision . . .

— Many of those who have returned are exiles at home.

XI

THE NEXT GENERATION

— Our young people are not the future—they are the present.

— By 1951 those of our young people who had survived had left Germany; but now we possess a new generation, born after the war. And suddenly it has ceased to be true to say that the Jewish community in Germany is old and dying.

— The parents are neither the German Jewish survivors, who are too old, nor their children, who are no longer Jews, but the DP's, and the middle-aged exiles who have returned with their children.

— . . . that most of them are the children of the 'foreign refugees'. Incidentally, Jewish communities in Germany have been populated by newcomers from Eastern Europe for the last 200 years. But it ought to be realised that their children, born and educated in Germany, no longer represent East European Jewry either in their language or their way of life.

— At the time of the liberation hardly any children survived in the concentration camps, and so today this age group is missing . . .

— The generation born immediately before and during the war is almost completely missing, so that there are fewer children . . . This is why the Jews in Germany must count on a large group of children of school age who will have appallingly few older companions.

— Hitler asked whether our parents or grandparents were Jews or half-Jews. What we ought to ask ourselves today is whether we are doing everything possible to ensure that our children will still be Jewish.

— For a short time after the liberation, a great deal was done for Jewish young people in Germany. Those who had survived were organised into groups, mostly in the vicinity of the camps, under the leadership of a few members of the old *Chalutz* movement and a few educators from Israel. Then they emigrated to Israel and other countries, and Germany was left once more without a Jewish youth movement. There followed some very barren years for the few young Jews who remained. The relief organisations and the newly-formed communities could at first do no more than attend to the most urgent needs; they had to help people to rebuild their lives. The youngsters grew up in alien surroundings, solitary and in isolation. There was hardly anyone to teach them Hebrew and religious knowledge; our few teachers were mostly old and poorly qualified.

— Twelve years after the war there are in the Federal Republic and West Berlin about 1,500 Jewish children of school age; there are more than 2,000 children up to the age of twenty. These young people present us with human and educational problems quite unlike those known to us from previous generations. Many of them still suffer from the effects of the Nazi persecution of their families; others know little or nothing about Judaism and have never known the security of Jewish family life. Too many of our children and adolescents still live under conditions which are far from normal and healthy. With the exception of Berlin and Munich, none of the communities have enough young people to make it possible to do very much for them. Only in these towns have regular activities for the young been organised.

We are slowly becoming aware that the Jewish community in Germany, impoverished in every respect and with too many old people, has the good fortune to possess a rising generation.

— That we have had no Jewish youth organisation has doubtlessly been responsible for the fact that about half of all the older adolescents living in Germany today have been lost to Judaism. They are no longer interested in being Jews and, under the circumstances, who would be able to make them change their minds? But we are convinced that they might have become good Jews . . .

— One does not need to be a prophet to be able to predict that, unless we can provide our children with some Jewish knowledge, they will within a few years have become so estranged from

Judaism that we cannot count on them to take any part in the activities of our community in the future. Already, one has only to glance into any synagogue to see that the children present can be counted on the fingers of one hand. Who will take the place of the dying generation? Let no one imagine that a child who spends 90 per cent and more of his day amongst non-Jewish influences, will be able of his own accord to become a good Jew, that he will ever become really interested in Jewish activities.

Our children are scattered all over Germany and have far too little contact with Judaism; this represents a threat not only to our communities but also to the spiritual welfare of the child.

— Very few of our communities provide religious instruction for the children of German-Jewish parents. Admittedly, the number of these children is rather small. There are far more children of East European parentage, but most of them have not yet reached school age. However, these children mostly belong to orthodox families and they are brought up within reach of the sources of Judaism—the Bible and the Talmud; for the other children, instruction in Jewish knowledge has been replaced by the teaching of Jewish history and information about Israel.

— The Jewish teachers working in Germany today possess the most diverse qualifications and experience. Some of them belong to the older generation of German Jews, who attended training colleges in Germany; others were trained in Israel or in Eastern Europe.

— Children may begin to attend Jewish religious instruction when they are between six and nine years old; finally this depends upon the parents. Most of them cease to attend after they have reached the age of thirteen and been confirmed. On the average, therefore, a Jewish child in Germany today receives a more or less regular religious education for between three and seven years; for many of them this is the sole opportunity in their whole life to study Jewish history, Jewish tradition, Hebrew and the Jewish religious beliefs.

— The youth centres were established primarily in order to encourage our young people to feel that they belong to the

Jewish community. A youth centre gives the young people the opportunity to meet other young Jews whenever they have the time, and so to establish closer ties within the community. The larger communities provide rooms, equipped to meet the needs of children of all ages. For some time now youth leaders, organisers and specialists have endeavoured to provide activities for the young.

— All these efforts made by the Jewish communities and organisations on behalf of the children were intended to ensure that the next generation would freely commit itself to remaining Jewish. Not infrequently, this raised the question of whether or not this ought to be the aim, because it may be doubted that Jews can continue to live in Germany without sacrificing their psychic health and their own humanity.

— The alien street, the alien school, the family life existing in a spiritual vacuum, the feeling of isolation—all these are dangerous for the psychic development of a child.

— Almost, it is a question of a 'second survival'. The communities of mainly old people need the young, and the young themselves are searching for obligations which will give a meaning to their lives.

— The Jewish families who came to live in Germany from Eastern Europe suffered not long ago such a disruption of their normal existence that the evidence of this trauma is apparent in their children today. The children suffer from psychic disturbances and other difficulties. They are faced with the problem of adjusting to unfamiliar surroundings. Their families are emotionally and financially insecure. Many of the children are faced with a sudden switch of languages.

These youngsters are torn between two worlds at a time of crisis in their personal development, and they react not only with a neurotic inability to learn but also with symptoms of the deepest anxiety.

Few of the children suffer from inhibitions; on the other hand, there are very many who are disturbed, aggressive, and insolent. Young children are most often disturbed, aggressive, anxious, and have problems at night; children of school age are more often unable to learn and have difficulties in their relationships with contemporaries and teachers; some of the adolescents suffer from inhibitions, others are extremely aggressive and show tendencies towards delinquency. More than half of the children in need of psychiatric treatment are Israelis.

— Those who have been brought here by their parents from somewhere in Europe or from overseas are used to being regarded as second-class citizens—as Jews, but those of us who have come from Israel feel that here we are being deprived.

— ... that this group tends to go to extremes, and suffers most from both external and internal conflicts. They grew up without being subjected to restrictions or prejudices for being Jews— on the contrary, they were taught to be proud of it; as Israelis they are self-assured and reject the diaspora. And now these young Israelis are living in just that country in which Jews have been most degraded, amongst just those people who subjected them to the worst treatment recorded in all their history. Against their own wishes, they were brought there by their parents who wanted to have a small share in Germany's prosperity. In consequence they feel humiliated, ashamed, inferior, and guilty. This sometimes shows openly, in conversation, and sometimes increases the Israeli superiority-complex and intensifies the rejection of Germany, and leads to grave problems generally both at home and at school.

That they learn with difficulty partly accounts for the extraordinarily low marks these Israelis tend to get for German. Because this subject epitomises the 'guilt' and so calls forth all their accumulated aggressive instincts: German identity is rejected, the German teacher is boycotted, his own guilty self is punished, and the parents are refused their moral justification for living in Germany, which they frequently try to find in their children's education. At the same time all this demonstrates their loyalty towards their Israeli ideals and towards their former educators—under the circumstances, the only protest open to the Israeli child living in Germany.

These children, who have until now known only the Israeli motto 'no more diaspora!' suddenly find themselves living in just that country of the diaspora against which every Jew is prejudiced. Their uncles and aunts may have fought to avenge those who died in the holocaust and to prepare the way for the Jewish State, but the patience, tolerance and adaptability which they themselves are expected to show towards the Germans were —according to Israeli opinion—what helped to lead six million Jews to their destruction.

— ... speech defects and frequently feelings of hatred and anxiety, because they have to live in a country whose population has caused their people so much suffering. In addition, there are the memories of the concentration camps, and with them the fear that it may all happen again.

— The Israeli children in Germany are, on the one hand, apparently integrated within the community of their German contemporaries; on the other hand, they most definitely reject the diaspora type of Jew and tend to idealise the free Israeli in his own country. If it were not for this idealisation, the young Israelis would be the most likely of all the Jewish children in Germany to leave the Jewish community and to assimilate amongst the Germans. (And indeed, many of these young people insisted that they had more in common with their German school fellows, and found it easier to establish relations with them, than with other young Jews.)

This dichotomy is a neurotic compromise between the desire to enjoy the material advantages of living in Germany and the dictates of their conscience to be loyal towards the members of their families who were murdered or else to the ideals of the State of Israel. It is not possible to ignore the symptoms of this neurosis, and an Israeli youth leader in Germany comments: 'The children are bewildered and disturbed; most of them need some sort of psychological treatment.'

— Their Jewishness is partly a vague, barely realised feeling and partly a distinctive and quite conscious awareness of belonging to the Jewish community.

— It is inevitable that we too, especially here in Germany, will become exposed to all the doubts and inner conflicts of previous generations.

— We don't want to pretend that our position is not much more difficult than that of our non-Jewish friends who are the same age. After the catastrophe, we found not only that all moral and material values were in ruin, but that the whole world of our forefathers had been extinguished, exterminated; and we young Jews have to find our own bearings in a world which truly is far from being the best of all possible worlds.

'German Jewry' is for us a historical reference.

Our parents, the generation who themselves experienced the last war and who escaped certain death, find it difficult to establish personal relationships with each other. They have had a lot of experiences, amongst them many which they will always remember. There is a gulf between Jews and Germans which it will not be easy to bridge. Only we young people may be able to help there, by trying all the time to act as a link.

— A tiny group of children and adolescents, whose daily lives, occupations, conversations and interests hardly differ from those of the millions of non-Jewish contemporaries among whom they live. They have non-Jewish companions and friends, they go to school with them, learn the same things from the same teachers, are influenced by the same books and ideas, they study with them in the same universities and like them take their place amongst German professionals. In what way are they Jews? They do not observe the religion in their daily lives; about 90 per cent keep neither the Sabbath nor the dietary laws; about 75 per cent rarely attend a synagogue service; their knowledge of the most basic tenets of Judaism is scanty and incomplete.

— We attend German schools, receive a German education; often our parents are themselves ignorant in Jewish matters. We become familiar with Germanic heroes, we listen to German music, read German literature; by training and by culture we are German. By the time we have grown up we are miles away from Judaism. I don't know if it is inevitable. But I have the feeling that our mentality adapts itself to our surroundings.

— Apparently young Jews find it more necessary to mix with the young Gentiles among whom they live than the other way round. To them, the Jewish community in Germany is a small

5

ghetto revolving continually in the same small circle; they want
to escape from it in order to make contact with events and
developments in the world at large.

— It can be a real friendship only when the other girl is also
Jewish, she will then be a companion come what may; the non-
Jewish friend allows a Jewish girl the vicarious satisfaction of
the gay, light-hearted and uninhibited life of the average German
adolescent.

— Of course what interests us most are our relationships with
boys. It is very sad for us that there is such a shortage of Jewish
boys. What few older boys there are—they are all about 19 years
old—consider themselves too grown up for a girl two or three
years younger, and anyway they seem to prefer the company of
German girls. But for a Jewish girl to go out with a non-Jewish
boy has always been considered unsuitable. Most of the girls
obey their parents in this respect, which is far from easy. It rules
out any possibility of being taken out to dances or to tea. A girl
risks her reputation if she breaks this taboo and does go out with
a non-Jewish boy, even if he is a neighbour or someone she goes
to school with . . .

— As soon as they reach adolescence, the desire to belong
becomes so strong that the internal conflict becomes almost
unbearable.

That they call this very human conflict between head and
heart 'typically Jewish' also proves that Jewish youngsters feel
themselves to be different from the others; the desire to break
away, to be free and light-hearted like other people, is opposed
from within them by all that they have inherited from their
forefathers. A really good youth movement could be of great
help to the individual, not only in finding a solution to this conflict but also in finding a suitable marriage-partner; and doubtlessly this was one of the considerations which has prompted
the various communities to establish youth clubs and youth
centres.

— The neglected memorial on the site of the former concentration camp Bergen-Belsen has been restored and decorated with

flowers by German soldiers; they have also tidied the graveyard. During manoeuvres on the Luneburger Heath they visited the camp site, and were shocked to find it in such a neglected condition.

— Twelve years after the war, two thousand young people made a pilgrimage to the heath; they were looking for Anne Frank. They found, not a single grave, but the earth piled up everywhere. They must then have felt something of the extent of the Jewish catastrophe, and on a marvellous impulse scattered their flowers all over the ground—there were flowers everywhere . . .

— Millions have seen the dramatisation on stage or screen of the 'Diary of Anne Frank'. It has become the tradition to visit the mass graves of the former concentration camp Bergen-Belsen, where this Jewish girl was one of the victims. Instead of trying to ignore the graves out there on the heath—as was indeed done for a long time—young people now put flowers on these graves. And so the individual fate of Anne Frank has become a bridge to the realisation of what happened during the persecution.

— Young people who took part in the pilgrimage to Bergen-Belsen have now formed an 'Anne Frank Circle' within the Hamburg Society for Christian-Jewish Collaboration. Presumably other groups in other towns of West Germany will follow their example; these young people have made it their aim to foster friendly relations between young people of every denomination, but above all to encourage an exchange of ideas with young Jewish people in Germany and abroad.

✡ *The son shall not bear the iniquity of the father. (Ezekiel 18,20)*

— Our hope that Jews and Germans may one day be able to develop a natural relationship with each other rests entirely upon the next generation.

— It has become obvious over the past few years that young Germans have been so disillusioned with the Nazi regime because of the disgrace which it has brought upon their country, that they are unlikely to be influenced by its teachings.

— I have confidence in the next generation of Germans, but a
residue of National Socialism still poisons the atmosphere in
which they are growing up. It is quite obvious that the parent
generation does not want their children to be informed about the
events of the past.

— They wanted to know everything that their parents had
been keeping from them, and how these things could have
happened. They wanted to know, they asked questions, they
read books, they thought about it. When I returned for the first
time after twenty years, to the town to which both they and I
belonged, I talked to them. I told them, openly and honestly,
without being ashamed . . . And what until then had been nothing
but dry history to them, suddenly fired their imagination.

† *We can do nothing now to alter the past—but we can, we must
and we shall all of us do something towards a better future.*

† *We who are alive today cannot manage without this history.
No matter how much we may wish to ignore it. To master these
events, to make them a part of our own experience, for the sake of
the present and the future—that is something we can do, and we
must do it.*

— People are ready to say a lot of nice things about the young
Germans. They are supposed to be better, more decent, more
humane, more tolerant than their fathers. They are supposed to
be a critical generation who reproach their fathers with having
supported a despot like Hitler. They collect much praise, these
young Germans—but ought it not to be taken for granted that
they would condemn crimes like those of their fathers?

— The Germans feel that they owe the Jews something and
this feeling now and again causes young Germans to be genuinely
attracted to Judaism. This interest is beginning to seem almost
natural and inevitable.

† *As young Christians, we are often uncertain and afraid when we
are faced with anything Jewish. From earliest childhood we have
heard about the Jews, but few of us have had the opportunity to get
to know one of them. A synagogue service is for many of us still a
sort of mystic secret meeting. It is the general opinion that the Jews
want to keep themselves to themselves and to have as little as*

possible to do with their surroundings. In addition, there is the embarrassment caused by memories of the persecution, made worse because we have never been given a satisfactory explanation of it.

Last year I and eight other young German students spent some weeks working on a kibbutz; since then I am learning Hebrew. Together with a few Jewish and German friends we have founded German-Israeli study groups at many universities; their membership is not restricted to students. We try to arrange meetings and to spread information amongst young Germans. Again and again I have found that it is much easier for us to have a proper conversation with Israelis than with German Jews—but then, these are of course in a very difficult position.

— Once every discussion here between Jews and non-Jews was centred upon Germany, the fatherland, which was loved and admired, which was protected and defended, by Jews and non-Jews alike; things are very different today. Now the idea of Israel dominates every conversation or discussion, it is the focus of every argument; it is what comes between people and what brings them together.

Thousands of young Germans go to Israel in order to find out about the Jewish State and its population. When these young people meet a Jewish boy, they immediately label him according to their idea of Israel, even when this young Jew has nothing to do with that country apart from the fact that he is Jewish. And as soon as it becomes apparent that this is a Jew who does not have any connection with Israel, that he is without the security of country and home, the atmosphere changes and the old inherited idea of the Jews takes over.

— The young Germans may have changed in many ways—in one respect they have not changed at all: that is in their attitude to the Jews. Most people avoid using the word Jew; while 'Catholic' or 'Protestant' indicate membership of a certain religious group, the word 'Jew' has remained an insult.

— To find that there is nothing extraordinary about meeting a Jew, who may even speak their own language, comes to many young Germans as a shock. They look for the 'alien element' and

are satisfied when they find it. They have no defence against a
Jew who is just like one of them.

— Why do so many young Germans feel uncomfortable when
they meet young Jews? They feel uncomfortable—you can tell
by the way they behave, by the way they express themselves and
by their excessive reserve. Why do they have to discuss with us
subjects which thank God belong to the past? They constantly
try to justify themselves in their behaviour towards us—they
don't have to do that and we have no right to expect it of them.

— I know only one or two young Germans who regard me
simply and solely as a friend. All the others think of me first of
all as a Jew, who has to plead for their friendship, even for their
goodwill.

Of course one cannot expect every young non-Jew to have a
Jewish friend—there are not even enough young Jews in West
Germany to go round. And we do not expect to be loved as we
have in the past been hated. What we do expect of young
Germans is that they should concern themselves with the question of why those things happened, and how they could have
done. How could the German people commit such crimes? My
friend, the only German boy whom I can without hesitation call
my friend, confessed to me one day that his father too had been
one of these notorious SS-men, he explained to me how this
came about and told me that he was very sorry, and I had the
impression that this boy really had come to terms with the past.
On the one hand, there is his father, beloved and admired, whom
he does not want to disown, on the other hand there are the war
crimes, which he loathes and condemns. Certainly, he is German.
In spite of his father's prejudices, in spite of all hatred, he makes
friends with a Jew simply because he likes him. He still harbours
little bits of prejudices. He still believes the fairy-tale of Jewish
wealth. Every Jew has money, simply because he is a Jew . . .
He refuses to believe that there are also poor Jews. But in the
course of conversations, discussions and arguments, our relationship has developed into a normal, genuine friendship, uncom-
plicated and without suspicion.

— They find it difficult to accept me simply as a human being, with whom they have much in common . . . I am to them first of all the Jew, and only afterwards do they consider the fact that I am their age, and are willing to have something to do with me . . . This is not to say that they are again antisemitic. Rather, their attitude could be called philosemitism. But the mere fact that the relationship is not normal is a reproach to the young Germans —but also to the young Jews . . . We young Jews must remember that we can only do harm if we are hostile, reserved and shy. The young Germans have to regain confidence in Germany and in themselves before we can meet again on common ground . . .

XII

DESECRATIONS

— The desecration of cemeteries was not a Nazi invention; it has always been popular in Germany. But at no other time have so many graves been desecrated as in the years since Nazism is supposed to have been overcome.

— Never have so many tombstones been overturned in Germany as in the years since the collapse of the Nazi regime.

— The spirit of Auschwitz continues to live in those who do these things . . .

— That is how it begins and at the end of it there are the gas chambers.

— Again and again, our cemeteries are being desecrated: it is a short step from having no respect for the dead to ill-treating the living, and again, it is a short step from there to Auschwitz. We know from our own experience where it can lead to once people cease to behave like human beings.

— Although these transgressions can no longer disturb the dead, they interfere with the peaceful co-existence of the different groups within the population and are therefore a threat to peace.

— . . . to consider the desecration of a cemetery not as an insult to this or that religion, but simply as a profanation of what is holy.

† *Every time a cemetery is desecrated, Germany loses a battle in its fight for a place amongst the nations. (Theodore Heuss)*

— One after another the cemeteries are being desecrated; there is no end to it. Again and again one hears of this sort of vandalism; it all contributes to Germany's bad reputation.

— Whenever Jewish cemeteries are desecrated, what matters is not so much their desecration as the desecration of the new Germany's good name.

— Not in deference to foreign opinion, but in deference to Germany's own best interests . . .

— Every right-thinking person here and all over the world is less concerned with the events themselves than with the new Germany's reaction to such events.

— The disinclination to investigate seriously the origin of such happenings is far more serious than the incidents themselves.

— 176 desecrations of Jewish cemeteries have taken place between 1945 and 1958; they are a symptom which cannot be ignored. This lack of respect for the dead, and also the fact that no one is ever called to account for these things, must unfortunately make one doubt the much-vaunted change of attitude.

✡ *Between 1948 and 1957, one-tenth of Germany's 1,700 Jewish cemeteries, most of which lie abandoned or are in isolated areas, were vandalised, in 93 per cent of the cases by juvenile delinquents, about half of whom knew that these were Jewish cemeteries. (The number of Christian ones desecrated in the same period was somewhat higher, but comparatively, of course, lower.)*

— Statesmen and diplomats are of course right when they draw attention to the fact that the number of Germans who commit antisemitic outrages is small, and that the overwhelming majority of the people want to have nothing to do with these happenings. But the few terrorists are active precisely because millions of peace-loving Germans have been more or less corrupted by antisemitism. And this means that when the cemeteries are desecrated, those responsible are not the few perpetrators but the millions of Germans who, without desecrating cemeteries, subscribe to some sort of antisemitism or lack the courage to make a resolute stand against it. These millions so to speak secretly commission the others to desecrate the cemeteries.

— I don't think we should regard these demonstrations of anti-semitism as individual manifestations of personal hatred or revenge. Tombstones are not damaged in order to offend the Jews who cherish these particular graves or those who may visit the cemetery within the next few days, but for the sake of getting it into the newspapers. If it is reported in the newspapers, it will

5*

first of all encourage every antisemite in the country and incite him also to demonstrations, and secondly it will give the Jews the feeling of being persecuted, and thirdly it will intimidate every right-minded German and convince him that politics continue to be determined by terror and violence.

— There can be no doubt that the desecration of Jewish graves and memorials is intended to frighten and intimidate the population. It is prompted by the wish to demonstrate that 'they' are still—or again—at work, that 'they' are watching and manipulating political opinion from behind the scenes . . . Finally, each desecration of a cemetery will be seen by the general population as a trial of strength between Nazism and democracy.

✡ *To attack Jewish cemeteries has even a sort of diseased logic: it is, after all, the dead Jews rather than the living who lie with such a crushing weight of accusation on Germany's claim to equality of esteem.*

— The police has been criticised for not proceeding with sufficient determination whenever a Jewish cemetery has been desecrated; in fact a special department has been established to deal with the investigation of these cases. It is claimed that in 15 cases out of 20 during the past two years, children at play were responsible for the desecration. It is further claimed that in spite of every effort made, the other cases have remained unsolved.

— We have appealed to the police; in some cases the chief of police himself has led the investigation. But always inquiries have led to the conclusion that those responsible were children, of various ages and frequently from bad homes. There is no reason to suspect that these things are organised; so far, no one has succeeded in providing a satisfactory explanation.

— Apparently children in Germany today no longer play with marbles but with tombstones, and are as strong as the giants were of old.

— On the few occasions when those responsible have been caught they have always been children, said to have accidentally trespassed on a Jewish (always a Jewish) cemetery while picking berries or playing hide-and-seek. The present case is certainly not accidental, as a wall several feet high separates the cemetery from a very busy street. And the tombstones certainly did not fall down because some child carelessly stumbled against them. The oldest of the children who has been caught was seven years old when the war ended, the youngest was three. And so it is out of the question to hold the Nazis responsible for what these children have done. On the other hand, we cannot very well hold them responsible, either. There is only one alternative: either these children are brought up in such a way that they regard the desecration of Jewish graves as a game, or someone told them to do it.

— There is again talk of 'children at play'—what sort of up-bringing must these children have? Has it not been pointed out again and again that it is important to the future of this country that its children should be brought up in a responsible manner?

— If nothing is holy to them while they are children, what about the future German adults?

— Again and again, the attempt has been made to represent these events as the unrelated deeds of irresponsible elements or as the pranks of some naughty youngsters. This warfare against the dead is really directed against the living. Either the Germans have an ineradicable tendency to desecrate cemeteries, or the police force is so riddled with former Nazis that it is not interested in preventing or punishing this sort of crime.

— We are in all this less concerned for the small Jewish community than for Germany itself and for the world, whose peace is threatened by the very existence of such maniacal tendencies. Today, a vague fury vents itself under cover of darkness against silent graves. Perhaps tomorrow the long-repressed energy of future concentration camp guards will find other objectives. In the long run, of what value are the declarations of elder statesmen, when the police throws the blame for the desecration of Jewish cemeteries on the next generation, to whom after all the future is supposed to belong?

— On Christmas Eve, in the night from 24th to 25th December 1959, the recently consecrated new synagogue in Cologne was desecrated with slogans and swastikas. This initiated a wave of

antisemitic and fascist activities in West Germany which reached
its climax two weeks later. On 7th January 1960 alone, 58 such
incidents were reported.

— On Christmas Eve, two men in their early twenties defiled
the outer wall of the synagogue in Cologne with the slogans
'Jews get out!' and 'Germans demand: Jews get out!' At the
same time, they daubed with black oil paint a slogan on the
monument to the victims of fascism. These two outsiders have
been enthralled by National Socialist doctrines and propaganda,
although during the Nazi era they were still too young to know
anything about politics. Their action, by arousing the majority of
Germans to genuine indignation, has received an extraordinary
amount of publicity, which has spread the infection and stimu-
lated others equally misguided to imitate them.

— Following the incidents in Cologne, similar desecrations in
all parts of West Germany had reached the total of 685 by 28th
January 1960, including 215 scribblings by young children. This
breaking of the rules, this rebellion against the taboo in force
since the end of the war, became a psychosis by which both
young and old were affected. Those discovered to be responsible
for 234 antisemitic and fascist incidents included 35 children up
to the age of 14; 95 youngsters and adolescents between the ages
of 14 and 20; 49 between 20 and 30 years old, 22 between 30 and
40 years old, 16 between 40 and 50 years old, 11 people between
50 and 60 years, and 6 people above the age of 60.

There were further incidents after 28th January 1960. But the
psychosis died down relatively quickly.

— It would not be true to say that we were startled or surprised. People who have had our experiences have so to speak
acquired a certain immunity. We had induced in ourselves some
sense of security, and we have had to wake up. And now we have
become aware of feelings which we had obviously only suppressed.

— We are today confronted with events which need surprise
no one except those who refuse to admit that the threat has been
developing quite logically over the years. We ourselves are not
surprised, and note for the record that there was a touch of

prophecy in our analysis of the situation. But the older people among us have been badly shaken. Much damage has been done which can never be repaired. How passionately they believed in Germany's change of heart when they returned from exile!

— More than fourteen years after the war the eternal question: 'To go or to stay?' is still—or again—topical.

— You will no doubt understand that many Jews living in Germany have been most deeply hurt. On Christmas Day, I witnessed the most heartbreaking scenes in front of the synagogue in Cologne. A number of Jewish citizens had collected there, shocked and thoroughly alarmed; these people had lost all their relations during the Hitler regime, they had returned to Germany because they believed that they would be able to live here again in spite of everything. They wept at the thought that they would now once more have to uproot themselves. Unlike us, they had deluded themselves during the past few years that there would never again come a day on which they would feel homeless on German soil.

— Desecrated cemeteries and signs of antisemitism, these were the hard facts confronting many a returning exile. And the children whom they brought with them experienced in their young hearts the deepest disappointment; they blamed their parents most bitterly.

— Now all these people are asking what the future may hold for them. It is worst when old people ask if they will be allowed to die in peace. Because for them another emigration is out of the question. On the other hand, to the young people, especially to those who were brought here by their parents from Israel, it is no problem. Because they will anyway one day decide to return to Israel, especially if there should ever be a repetition of the events of the past few weeks. They are not frightened. They merely blame their parents for having brought them here. They have no real understanding of what their parents have been through. And there are also people who still say: 'We are good Germans, we shall not leave this country.' They are like those who wanted to remain in Germany even after 1938. There are not many, but there are some like that. They blame those of us who think differently for becoming excited, they say that we help to poison the atmosphere.

—   What happened on Christmas Eve and the sequel frightened the Jews abroad much more than those who are living here—because the Jews abroad did not regard the incidents as local.

—   At the moment, we are not threatened by any immediate danger. A crisis always looks different, that is milder, seen from close by than it does from a distance.

—   If necessary we will have the strength to live not merely in this environment but in spite of it, and we will rouse the right people now, today, everywhere and in every walk of life, so that the catastrophe may not repeat itself.

—   We neither want to convert the Nazis nor to change the attitude of those guilty of crimes against humanity. We are concerned with our own attitude.

—   One of the reporters asked: 'Rabbi, what would you do with those two men, Strunk and Schoenen?' And the rabbi answered: 'I would invite them to tea and talk to them.'

—   In Berlin they also painted slogans and fascist symbols on the walls, but these certainly did not have the intended effect. Especially some of the schools, the youth organisations, the students' union and every institution concerned with the young worked harder than ever to propagate the idea that in a free and tolerant democracy Jews ought to be considered equal citizens, and to persuade people to be sincerely willing to accept them as such.

—   The spontaneous demonstration by young people in West Berlin against the appearance of antisemitic slogans in Cologne was a rebellion of the German conscience.

—   Last week, tens of thousands of youngsters, students and adults in West Berlin demonstrated against antisemitism and neo-fascism. By torchlight they marched in silence through the streets. Amongst the demonstrators were members of the West Berlin Senate, representatives of all the parties and of the trade unions.

—   The Federal Republic Youth Circle has asked its members —six million young people of all parties and denominations—

and indeed all young Germans to fight against every manifestation of antisemitism, so that the rising German generation may
not be identified with 'hooligans who paint slogans on walls'.

† *On Monday, 18th January 1960, delegates of 20 students' and
youth organisations belonging to various political movements and
denominations convened in Munich. They passed a unanimous
resolution protesting against the antisemitic incidents and resolving
to take positive counter-measures. They pledge you their unanimous
support. (Telegram of the Munich youth organisations to the
Central Council of Jews in Germany)*

† *The passionate arguments released amongst the German
population by the recent manifestations of antisemitism have resulted
in liberating the relationship between Jews and non-Jews in Germany
from the petrification from which it has suffered since the end of
the persecution. Thanks to the recent manifestations of antisemitism,
crowds are marching through the streets on an impulse to demonstrate
against incidents which, according to the government's White Paper,
are in fact unimportant and of no political significance. And thanks
to them, the Federal Diet has been induced to discuss openly and in
public the relationship between Jews and Germans and to say
outright what until now no one has dared even to whisper.*

† *In the midst of the world's vehement and voluble reactions to the
incidents of the past few weeks, there has begun between Germans
and Jews a sort of silent dialogue which indicates, in spite of everything, a secret sense of community.*

— When the first shock was over, things made a very different
impression. Never before have so many people—even complete
strangers—reassured us unasked that they condemn all signs
of antisemitism and anybody responsible for them. They vied
with each other in private, personal demonstrations of kindness
and sympathy. All of us without exception received so many
spontaneous expressions of personal affection from the people
around us, that we were almost overwhelmed by them. This
affection—I have to admit it—took us by surprise and filled us
with a glad hope; in the final analysis, it was much more characteristic than the painting of a few slogans by some people with a
need to attract attention.

— Over a hundred of those responsible were caught—and more than half of them not by the State but by private citizens who felt enraged and often formed neighbourhood squads. Most of those caught were adolescents; the sentences passed on them by the courts were much too severe.

— I have heard and read some very interesting things since Christmas. I am referring to the many letters and telegrams which I have received. I am not thinking so much of the official telegrams which were sent, but of the reactions from private individuals. Many—most—of them expressed a fellow-feeling with us. I was often moved—sometimes almost to tears—when I received small sums of money which represented their savings from children who wanted to express their sympathy, or when I received a letter from an old man who sent some money although he has eight children and is unemployed. These were people who really managed to express their feelings. And this is what reassures me, what even makes me feel optimistic enough not to lose faith in humanity.

— The Jewish community in Cologne, the Central Council of Jews in Germany, numerous other Jewish organisations and communities as well as the weekly Jewish newspaper, the *Allgemeine*, have received telegrams and letters expressing indignation at the recent manifestations of antisemitism and solidarity with the Jews in Germany, from all sorts of German organisations and from individuals in every walk of life. Many Germans sent donations to the offices of Youth Aliyah in Frankfurt, including some for whom these meant a genuine financial sacrifice, in order to express their fellow-feelings for the Jewish people.

— As a result of recent events, the Societies for Christian-Jewish Collaboration in many towns have received letters and telephone calls, and some of the Societies report an influx of applications for membership from citizens representing a cross-section of the German population.

† *That this could have happened in our country here and now is a disgrace, which is not altered by the fact that in other countries walls were also painted with slogans against the Jewish people and with*

swastikas. Elsewhere fascism has caused unpleasantness, but only here has it led to the extermination of six million Jews.

† *Anyone who today at the age of 25 paints a swastika on a wall betrays his own ignorance. For this, either his parents or his teachers must be held responsible.*

† *Any thinking person ought to possess enough intelligence and common sense to realise quite clearly that one cannot hurt the Jews in this way without at the same time hurting the Germans, and we will find it much more difficult to recover from this injury than those for whom it was meant. Whether or not those responsible realised the significance of their action makes no difference, they were committing a crime.*

† *We ought at last to have finally realised that what happens to the Jews and what happens to the Germans is so closely interrelated that the sufferings of the one people are reflected upon the other. What we Germans need is peace within and without. These events have threatened our peace.*

† *Those responsible have been caught, the swastikas have been scraped away, the police receives a recommendation—from Federal President to burgomaster, everybody sends a telegram. That is the official reaction to the disgrace of Cologne. It is not enough. It is not enough because all this may be taken for granted, the telegrams, the being ashamed, the being sorry, the apologies. It is not enough because from Bonn to Dusseldorf there runs, through the reaction of the German Federal Republic, an undercurrent of sensitivity to world opinion: 'My God, what an impression this will make abroad!' Of course the effect is disastrous. But is that what matters? Is it not more important that we should examine ourselves, which we ought to have done long ago and still keep putting off?*

We are much too inclined to take the easy way out. Everybody who is asked to comment says: They are exceptions, they are muddle-headed, they are fanatics, but we—we are good Germans, we have always been good Germans, and there is no connection between these people and ourselves. What happened in Cologne is so disgraceful, that to take pride in the quick arrest of the perpetrators is very cold comfort indeed.

† *I wonder if it has occurred to any member of the government,*

that what happened in Cologne was a logical continuation of many another political manifestation in the Federal Republic?

—   It is not surprising that things like those in Cologne happen, considering that people with a questionable past are prominent on the political scene in Germany and spread Nazi propaganda openly and without consequences to themselves, and that young people read publications like the *Soldatenzeitung* with pronounced antisemitic and fascist tendencies. It is alarming how many right-wing youth organisations there are in the Federal Republic and in West Berlin.

†   *The outside world gets to hear of the desecrations. But it has other, even better reasons for being distrustful and suspicious of us. According to our information, what receives the most attention on the far side of our borders is whether we treat these incidents as trifles, or whether we give them the serious attention they deserve. The real danger to us is that we assess them as matters of little importance . . . The world will watch to what extent we have regained our national self-respect.*

XIII

ANTISEMITISM

✡ *Whether they lived or whether they died made no difference; people always said 'he is a Jew'. (Jakob Wassermann)*

† *It is not their experience with Jews which influences people's idea of them, but their prejudices which colour their experience. If there were no Jews the antisemites would have to invent them.*

Antisemitism is not an opinion or a point of view, but a question of disposition.

Antisemitism is fear of the common lot of humanity.

Tell me whether you are an antisemite, and I will tell you whether you are human. (Jean Paul Sartre)

— The word antisemitism was coined by a German writer about 80 years ago and has since been in general use as a pseudo-scientific expression denoting opposition to Jews.

† *The root of race-hatred which is almost an instinct is fear of the —unfamiliar. What is unfamiliar is incalculable, incommensurable; and what is incalculable may become dangerous. Antisemitism sees in the Jews a sort of secret society. (Bertrand Russell)*

— Antisemitism creates the idea of a group of people whose very existence is their guilt, who are not individually responsible and therefore cannot demand to be treated as individuals.

† *It is an essential part of antisemitism to hold a whole minority responsible for each of its members.*

† *Antisemitism begins where the individual is treated in a collective way as 'the Jew'.*

† *Antisemitism, by the way, is not an idea. Above all it is a passion.*

† *Antisemitism is uncharitableness and hatred.*

† *Antisemitism resulted in the destruction of the conscience.*

† *Every superstition and delusion makes use of a cruel trait of human nature—the instinct of the chase.*

† *Antisemitism implies more than the extermination of the Jews. Antisemitism implies plain misanthropy.*

† *It is quite simply not true that there exists a good and sufficient cause for antisemitism; it exists without cause. Every reason which is advanced to justify it has been an afterthought. The true origins of antisemitism are superstition, delusion, xenophobia, and intolerance of neighbours and fellow-citizens who wish to live in their own, special way.*

† *During the Middle Ages a Jew could escape his fate through having himself baptised. For the contemporary Jew this is no longer a way out. Today it is not so much the religion which is resented as the race, and not so much the race as the Jew simply as a Jew.*

† *. . . objecting not to the individual and not to the group, but to the type. This comes about through the naturalistic attempt to see people impersonally, through the tendency of the industrial society to turn individuals into objects. The absurdity of it all becomes particularly apparent when the instinctive antisemite actually encounters a Jew. This Jew is always seen as the exception which proves the rule. When a Jew is actually encountered, the typical image collapses.*

† *Anybody looking today with open eyes at the history of the past 30 years must realise that antisemitism is merely the first symptom of the onset of a terrible psychic illness affecting a whole people.*

† *Antisemitism did not necessarily have to lead to the gassing of men, women and children; it ought to be treated as a symptom of an inferiority complex rather than as a crime.*

† *Antisemitism is not directed against individual Jews, but against the typical image of the Jew. And this typical image would continue to exist, even if not a single Jew remained within reach of the Germans, indeed, it would continue to exist if every Jew were to disappear from the face of the earth.*

† *At last it has been proved that antisemitism is not caused by the Jews; in fact, it does not need them at all.*

— The German Jews are dead; German antisemitism is still very much alive.

— It was not invented by Hitler, and the idea of it remained virulent after all outward signs of it disappeared with the defeat of the Nazis.

— To the question: 'Is there still antisemitism in Germany today?' the answer will have to be: 'Yes, there is.' According to the polls held at regular intervals by German institutes researching into public opinion, between 25 and 34 per cent of those asked openly admit to being antisemites. That is, roughly speaking, between a quarter and a third of the population.

† *I believe that Germans who have known pre-Hitler times (over 60) are immune to the new antisemitism and I am optimistic about the young people. But ordinary Germans between 35 and 60 find it hard to acknowledge that Hitler was a criminal. They feel mis-understood. They demand approval—they don't want to think that everything they fought and suffered for was wrong. They say: Hitler made great mistakes, but ...*

— It must be admitted that some degree of antisemitism in Germany is understandable and has to be expected. Actually, I am rather surprised how little one finds of it in daily life. After all, a whole generation of Germans were brought up and educated under the Nazis and came under the influence of their very clever propaganda and press. It is highly unlikely that no trace of it should have remained.

— Most people are not interested in their Jewish neighbours. But an occasional conversation will show that their attitude towards the Jews is still determined by the same old prejudices.

— Most certainly we have not cherished the illusion that after twelve years of indoctrination, Germany would suddenly be free of antisemitism and Nazis.

— They have been so thoroughly poisoned that it is inevitable that some of them should resist re-education.

— If we don't want to deceive ourselves we will have to admit that the Germans have been very thoroughly indoctrinated with antisemitism.

— On the contrary, it would be surprising if every Nazi without exception had in the meantime changed his mind and become a reasonable, moderate and tolerant citizen.

✡ *If there were no more antisemitism in Germany I would be highly suspicious. A country cannot so easily dissolve its connection with its past.*

— It would be naive of any Jew to believe that the very people who a short while ago pursued or profited by the final solution have suddenly today become our friends.

— We must hope that antisemitism will die out with the older generations.

— I would like to think that the present signs of antisemitism are only the aftermath of the antisemitism which existed until 1945.

† *We must not underestimate the amount of antisemitism there is today, but we must also not overrate its possible consequences.*

† *Doubtlessly, there is more antisemitism in Germany than any-where else. This has become apparent in the past, and it is the past which determines the present attitude of the Jews to the Germans. Age plays an important part here.*

† *It is a long-established fact that people have a tendency to hate those towards whom they feel guilty. The crimes which the Germans have committed against the Jews will not let them rest and make them even more antisemitic than they were before.*

† *Probably, German antisemitism today is very much bound up with German guilt or the question of German guilt—a question which has never been settled. People hear of what happened during the persecution, perhaps they themselves took an active part in it, perhaps they are innocent—anyway, this guilt exerts a terrible pressure on them which could easily lead to antisemitic incidents.*

† *. . . the question of whether this is in fact a 'genuine' anti-semitism—that is: whether it has to do with ourselves rather than with the Jews, with our sense of guilt which we cannot come to terms with, with our injured pride, with being ashamed of ourselves . . .*

† *But this is not a genuine antisemitism in as much as it consists of a vague mixture of complexes which have been suppressed, a bad conscience which is being ignored and a sense of our own inadequacy which we have to fight again and again.*

† *Perhaps we are all of us still convalescing, like people after a long illness. I don't know what will happen afterwards. But while the body has not yet quite recovered, while the temperature is not yet quite normal, we cannot really assess the situation. The only thing*

*I am quite sure about is that we have not yet got beyond this stage
today.*

† *I don't think that the phrase antisemitism without Jews is very
well chosen. Firstly, a few Jews still remain in Germany; to the
muddle-headed antisemites those few are indulging in riotous living
at our expense—by means of the reparation payments. Secondly,
the amount of the reparations paid to the Jews in Germany, in
Israel, all over the world, is imagined by these dim-wits to be im-
measurable and immense, an extortion of German national wealth.
And thirdly: even if not a single Jew remained in Germany today,
it would still not be correct to talk about an antisemitism without
Jews, because we have saddled ourselves with such a burden of moral
guilt that in thought, as pangs of conscience, the whole of Jewry is
with us in Germany today. The antisemitism of today feeds on the
past and is aimed at the future.*

† *The very word Jew is of incalculable significance. Nobody is
left unaffected by it. One person will respond to it with horror,
because of the sufferings which the Jews have had to bear, while
another will feel uncomfortable when he hears it. Inevitably, the
reaction to it will be an emotional one. I think the words 'Jew' and
'Jewish' are dangerous, because people are never quite sure what
they themselves mean by them. The past has loaded the word Jew
with a tremendous charge, one could almost say it has loaded it with
horror.*

† *There are other countries with a longer tradition of antisemitism, but in Germany it celebrated its most horrible triumphs. A
vague sense of sharing the responsibility and the guilt, of having
been wrong, of being involved, has resulted in a public taboo strictly
observed by most of the population, which in spite of everything is
far from independent. What today often claims to be antisemitism is
in reality not the genuine thing at all, but an attitude originating in a
mixture of these suppressed and depressing feelings from the
frightfulness of which one cannot escape.*

† *That is precisely what is so terrible, that there were not all that
many antisemites in Germany and yet it was possible for these things
to happen.*

† *It is paradoxical, and that is what makes it so terrible, that in*

other countries antisemitism has gone and still goes much deeper, but though there it has led to pogroms, it has never reached the stage of a thoroughly organised and systematically pursued extermination . . . we must concern ourselves with it, not to find excuses, but to realise what happened and to find an explanation, the reasons for it.

— Every manifestation of antisemitism reopens many old wounds, and rouses all over again memories of the exterminations.

† *Occasionally, an antisemite is nowadays defined loosely as a person who would like to see a repetition of the Nazi mass murders. This is not a reasoned definition and does not apply to the serious antisemite of today.*

✡ *Hitler has rid antisemitism of the respectability it enjoyed in many strata of German society. He made it a byword not only of defeat but of gas ovens and ghetto raids. Antisemitic survivors recently professed that they were 'definitely not antisemitic', to dissociate themselves from the mass murders committed in the name of antisemitism. Whatever they called mass extermination, it did not correspond to their own antisemitic ideas.*

— There can be no return to a traditional 'innocent' antisemitism for the Germans.

To make light of the moderate, restrained antisemitism of today would be a big mistake. The crimes of the past grew out of a moderate antisemitism.

— One advantage which the Jews no doubt have over the majority of Germans is an instinct for danger, an ability to assess danger, a realisation that after Auschwitz 'a little antisemitism' is no longer possible, that even when it appears to be marginal it ought to be considered a danger signal.

— Even if it does not allow us to draw conclusions about the attitude of the population as a whole, it is a symptom of an intellectual and moral sickness still gnawing at the roots of a society.

— Antisemitism does not limit itself to attacking the Jews: it is the first sign of a misanthropic movement, taking its place amongst all the other 'anti'-movements which regard every minority as a danger. We must re-think our fight against antisemitism as a much more comprehensive fight against hatred intolerance, and totalitarianism.

— It ought finally to be realised that with a Jewish population of 30,000 without influence in political or economic life, Germany does not have and cannot have a Jewish problem. This means that antisemitic and fascist attacks are to a very large extent attacks against the foundations of German democracy.

— We are blamed for being over-sensitive, but it is only that we have a good nose for danger. We know that we are always the first target of any reactionary forces.

— I am always attempting to explain that perhaps we Jews are merely the front-line, that perhaps we are merely a barometer.

— It has always been like that; we Jews are the first but not the only victims of political degeneration.

— Because antisemitism, which has always been the starting point, is not ultimately directed against us Jews, but against the democratic policies of a state, against democracy itself.

— ... that antisemitism is so to speak only the seedbed or the training-ground for plain barbarity.

— For the Nazis, the point of antisemitism was terror for its own sake, they saw it as a means of exercising their power as a totalitarian state.

— We expect all anti-fascist parties to realise that antisemitism is a part of fascism.

— In the final analysis, every reactionary movement in Germany will inevitably be antisemitic, whether or not this is part of its official programme.

† *Every political movement in Germany ought to remember that fascism is always in effect antisemitic, and that antisemitism is always in effect fascist. Otherwise Germany will cut itself off from the world. (Kurt Schumacher)*

✡ *In other countries antisemitism is an expression of ignorance and bigotry. In Germany it is a weapon of hate against the world.*

— Even the smallest attack against the Jews, even the most unimportant incident and the least manifestation of antisemitic thought, is a malicious, treacherous blow against civilisation and humanity as a whole. We ought to realise this and act accordingly.

— Today we have antisemitism without Jews. It is a return to the type of thing that led to 1933 . . . The danger is not so much to the small surviving group of Jews, as to the German republic itself. It doesn't matter so much to us that they say 'Not enough Jews were gassed' but next time they may say 'Not enough Russians were killed', or Englishmen or Americans—and that endangers peace.

— . . . that the attack is once again first of all directed against the Jews. Perhaps in the end we are of no interest to them, but we are always the first to be affected and to suffer.

— It is no less evident than it was about fifteen years ago. It merely affects a much smaller number of Jews.

— Look, what I simply cannot understand is the fact that we are still considered a genuine problem—so few of us have returned to Germany and we no longer matter in any sphere of public life. It is this disparity which bothers us when we come across any sign of antisemitism.

✡ *Granted that most Germans have changed their minds about how Jews should be treated, how far have they progressed on the much longer path to changing underlying attitudes towards the Jews? Adenauer revealed this transitional stage very nicely, when he said that aid to Israel should go on not only as a moral duty but 'as a piece of practical politics, because Jewry is extraordinarily powerful in the world . . .'*

✡ *Even if the Germans were free from prejudices, they could not ignore it when someone is a Jew.*

† *The term 'Jew' has been replaced by 'Jewish citizen'.*

— People observe the Jews—and this attention itself represents a psychological victory for the Nazi criminals and their propaganda.

— Most frequently one encounters an unconscious antisemitism, culminating in the almost classical sentence: 'He's all right in spite of being a Jew'.

— . . . more and more cases of Jews being cursed, insulted, and threatened openly in the streets. The times when these aberrations were an exception are long past. Try to imagine what an effect these incidents must have on people whom just this race-hatred has deprived of their closest relations. It must make their whole world collapse, and it has cost them so many years of effort to rebuild it. And how can such people be expected to continue to try to live on reasonable terms with the Germans?

— We are reproached with having become hypersensitive—understandably enough by people who wish us well. We are startled when we hear the word 'Jew', feel insulted and remain implacable even when we discover that it was only some fishwife cursing and swearing with rage. We really ought to possess enough psychological insight to realise that she did not mean it or if she did, that what she said did not matter.

In the days when Jews were in the habit of tolerantly telling and listening to disparaging jokes about themselves—that is, long ago—we believed that the German people had such a high regard for human dignity that when one of them used the word 'Jew' as a swearword, we let it pass as a vulgar slip of the tongue. But experience has shown that on the contrary . . .

The Nazis disappeared, but not for ever. It is by no means certain that the sufferings of their own people have brought about any fundamental changes in their way of thinking. Once more they are marching and singing. And are we seriously expected to believe, once more, that they are entirely harmless? No! We have been warned and cannot help suspecting the worst when someone screams the word Jew, even when it is only out of stupidity—which is more dangerous than bad intentions.

— The Germans have not been re-educated, their ideas are just the same as before. Our children come and tell us that their schoolfellows say to them: 'A pity that Hitler forgot to gas you and your parents'. It seems to me that such remarks indicate that both teachers and parents have failed in their efforts to guide the children in the right direction. When the subject of the Jews is raised, the teachers often refuse to discuss it; the parents ignore it. But often, through certain comments, the parents pass their own prejudices on to their children. That even today non-Jews still become embarrassed when they meet a Jew shows how ineradicable these prejudices are.

— It seems to me that there is only one possible way to

counteract the German's endemic hatred of the Jews. We don't want any special treatment—not Himmler's sort, and not the sort that handles us with kid gloves and wants to put us in a show-case. The only right that I am willing to demand for us is the right to be human, to commit parking offences like other people, to pull a fast one over some unlucky chap when finally selling the old crock with all its secret faults, like other people; to be drunk at night and kick up a row in the street, or even to commit robbery with violence like other people—and yet to have those other people say: Meyer's the one who did it, not the Jew Meyer is the one who did it, the Jews have done it, all Jews commit robbery with violence, kick up a row in the street and commit parking offences. Not until then, it seems to me, will both the black and the white antisemitism disappear from Germany.

— We do not claim that there are no offenders among us. Antisemitism would not disappear if every Jew were a saint without fault or blemish. On the contrary, the antisemites would be even more furious with the Jews. After all, there is in this imperfect world nothing more annoying than a perfect human being.

— It is even possible that the time will come when a German antisemite will regard an Israeli as his equal, but will continue to want to exterminate the Jews, especially the German Jews. And then everybody will finally have to realise that it does not make sense to hate the Jews.

— It is important to us that we should no longer be made to feel that we are in a special position. Often enough, even Germans with the best intentions regard us as peculiar, as exceptions. What we want is no more and no less than equality with the Germans in everyday life.

— First *Jud Süss*, then sweet Jew—they should have allowed themselves a little more time.

✡ . . . *a thoroughly misguided, though most nobly motivated desire to make intellectual amends forbids them to find a book bad if its author is a Jew, a refugee or a member of the anti-Nazi resistance, or if it deals—sympathetically of course—with one of these three subjects . . . The relationship between Jews and Germans*

*will become much healthier when people will cease to be so very
afraid of spoiling it.*

— Today, when a Jew is socially successful, this is not usually
due to personal merit. Out of a widespread at least unconscious
tendency to feel that they ought to compensate Jewry as a whole,
many Germans around us show themselves ready to be
prejudiced in our favour.

— This general extrovert friendliness makes life easier for
those of us who are not over sensitive. But sensitive people find
it hard to bear.

— We don't want to be spoiled, we don't want privileges—
this favouritism, this special consideration also is an insult. We
want to be treated as equals by our equals.

— It seems to me that the present-day philosemitism, taken
literally, is meaningless, if only because many Germans have
never even seen a Jew.

✡ *As there are considerably more antisemites than Jews in
Germany today, it is easiest for the new philosemite to demonstrate
his attitude by fighting antisemitism. This negative phenomenon
receives more attention than the positive contribution of Judaism as
an intellectual and spiritual force.*

† *Antisemitism is possible only as long as there is philosemitism—
and vice versa. Both attitudes prevent people from regarding a Jew
as a human being amongst others.*

— Not every opponent of antisemitism is entirely without
fault. But at least he isn't an antisemite. And that—from the
point of view of social relations—is at least an advantage.

— It would of course be wrong to label as an antisemite anyone
who is not a pronounced friend of the Jews.

— And what is the real issue? Most definitely not the Jews who
continue to live in Germany. From a purely practical point of
view, we have become unimportant, in a way we have become
no more than a symbol. I have to admit that it is not altogether
pleasant to be a symbol.

— We feel no more than tolerated, there are signs of renewed
antisemitism and the past is still much too close—everything
considered, I have to ask myself how Jews can possibly have the

courage to continue to live in Germany, and not merely to live there but to rebuild the synagogues, which are after all meant not so much for us as for future generations.

†   *While people have no Jewish neighbours to talk to, it is very difficult for them to change their old ideas about the Jews. Although not the Jews but the non-Jews have the responsibility of curing Germany of antisemitism, the absence of Jews makes it much more difficult to effect such a cure.*

Opinion polls have shown that the incidence of antisemitism among the population is in inverse proportion to the number of Jews who once lived in a district. Even today, antisemitic tendencies are still comparatively widespread and strong in the villages and small towns which never had a Jewish population, whereas in the towns which used to have large Jewish communities there is today hardly any antisemitism at all.

This antisemitism (without Jews) no longer represents a real threat to the Jews. But it is a very grave threat to non-Jews, because it corrupts those who succumb to it.

—   I think that the most important contribution which the Jews themselves could make would be not to hate in return for being hated. But the beginning of the problem has been and remains antisemitism, this hatred existing all over the world where the population is considered to be Christian. That is why I think that Christians are the ones who have to fight antisemitism.

—   ... that the chief difficulty is that the antisemites attack Jews as Jews, while the democrats defend them as human beings.

—   For us Jews, the problem remains unsolved; our non-Jewish neighbours have the problem of solving it.

—   In this day and age German antisemitism can do little harm to the Jews. But it can do a great deal of harm to the Germans.

—   Here and now, antisemitism is not a Jewish but a German problem.

—   Antisemitism is one of the signs that fascism still exists in Germany. Therefore, to combat it ought to matter much more to every single German than to any Jew.

†   *That the Germans should in all sincerity cease to be antisemitic*

*is much more important for their own future than it is for the future
of the Jews.*

†   *We Germans must overcome our antisemitism, not for the sake
of the Jews but for our own sake.*

XIV

THE PAST

— . . . that people were unhesitatingly killed because they were Jews. I am not saying 'merely because they were Jews'—it is no mere thing to be a Jew.

†   *Hitler gave us cause to be ashamed: and thus there arose a feeling of collective guilt.*

†   *There is no such thing as a 'collective guilt' of the Germans for the deportation and extermination of the Jews, but that these things will be connected with the name of Germany always, has burdened us with a collective sense of shame. (Theodor Heuss)*

†   *Something like a collective sense of shame has arisen out of the memory of those times, and remains. The worst thing Hitler did to us —and he did us much harm—was to oblige us to be ashamed to be, like him and his henchmen, Germans.*

†   *Am I, are you, are we guilty, because we were living in Germany at that time, do we share the guilt? The phrase 'collective guilt' and what it implies are a simplification, it is the reversal of the kind of attitude which the Nazis used to employ towards the Jews: that because they were Jews it followed that they were guilty. (Theodor Heuss)*

†   *If there was even one single German who was not guilty—and there were a few—one cannot talk of a collective guilt. And yet there cannot be such a thing as a general absolution.*

— Of course the term collective guilt does not brand every single German as personally guilty. But the word indicates that those who are passive spectators at such a tragedy are not innocent. Spectators of this sort have always been the world's greatest misfortune.

✡   *Those who do evil are guilty, and guilty, especially before the judgement of history, are all those who see or know of a crime being committed and keep quiet; it is they who, unintentionally, prepare the way for it. (Leo Baeck)*

† *Anyone who took no action against this antisemitism shares the guilt. Even when, indeed especially when he regarded this anti-Jewish superstition with amused contempt. He is guilty of not helping to prevent the humiliation, degradation and ruin which has befallen every one of us including himself.*

† *We demand that our people should admit its guilt.*

† *To have become guilty means to have purchased at a high price a deeper understanding of things.*

† *The six million dead are our dead. (Erich Lueth)*

† *At the end of the war, we may have been more aware of our guilt and we may have felt more passionately ready to atone, but on the other hand we were at the same time much less whole-hearted about it.*

— If the Germans ever want to be rid of their guilt we will have to have evidence that the overwhelming majority of them at least in retrospect condemn the crimes committed by the Nazis.

† *If the Germans want to become a democratic people they must never forget Auschwitz. (John McCloy)*

† *No one can fight fascism without at the same time mourning its victims. (Kurt Schumacher)*

† *The 30,000 Jews who are living in Germany today are no problem for us, but the six million dead are an enormous problem. (Erich Lueth)*

† *The past has its own laws which do not offer us a choice.*

† *When a nation endeavours to discard the legacy, good or bad, which it has inherited from its past and pretends to have no history, it ceases to be viable as a community. To dare to admit that we have committed crimes against the Jews has therefore become almost a proof of genuine and sincere patriotism.*

† *For years the Germans have done their best not to come face to face with their own inadequacy, and doubtlessly this is the reason why they have tried to avoid even to mention the Jewish problem until now. In this silence, obstinacy plays perhaps only a small part; by far the greater part of it is due to shame.*

† *Many people have long subscribed to the opinion that we ought to let the past rest, that the old wounds ought finally to be allowed to heal. But this is precisely what is so dangerous, precisely what*

might lead to conditions in which the past might well be able to repeat itself. We must not allow the old wounds to heal, we must not even cover them up . . . We need to be reminded of the holocaust continuously if we ever want to get it out of our system.

† *Common decency commands us to talk about the past.*

† *Even today there are sceptics who reject reality and refuse to acknowledge history itself; and these still maintain that the concentration camp murders are merely a malicious invention.*

† *. . . until every one of our children has been taught to understand that it is not a question of whether six or three million have been killed but whether even one Jew has been killed or not.*

† *It almost seems as if many of our countrymen are not yet ready to forgive the Jews for what the Germans have done to them.*

— They are annoyed with the Jews for reminding them all the time by their very existence of the darkest chapter in German history.

✡ *The attempt to excuse the inexcusable gives rise to a tendency to make the victim appear in an unfavourable light, so that it is the murdered and not the murderers who become the guilty ones.*

— In the end, we become annoyed with people whom we have wronged, because without meaning to they act as a reminder and continue to bother our conscience. That is why the victims of the persecution are again being insulted, why the reparation payments are looked at askance, why people try to blame the Jews for what was done to them—the Germans are merely trying to convince others but even more to convince themselves that they were quite right to put the Jews into concentration camps.

— Now there is nobody who was responsible for those terrible twelve years. Nobody took part in the persecution, nobody had neighbours whose flats were seized and no one suspected that the owners were being deported to Auschwitz or Theresienstadt; nobody remembers going to Jewish acquaintances to take charge in good time of their valuables for which anyway they would now have no further use.

And so, after the collapse of their military and political forces, there followed the collapse of their morality.

✡ *He is guilty because he looked the other way.*

† *I heard the name Belsen for the first time in the spring of 1945.*
(Theodor Heuss)
† *Nobody knew—I have been told again and again—maybe, but
the truth is that nobody wanted to know anything.*
† *The war was over, the Nazis were gone, the Germans became
self-accusing philosemites; each of them had his Jew whom he had
secretly saved, and none of them had ever heard of the concentration
camps . . .*
— The Jew cannot bear witness, he is dead.
— People who under Hitler had shown compassion towards the
persecuted Jews, now became neutral and impersonal. Conditions had changed, now many of them felt that they themselves
were being persecuted or innocently oppressed. The circumstances no longer appealed to their better feelings, the subject
was of no further importance to them.
— The death of one person is a misfortune, the death of ten
people is a tragedy, the death of a hundred people is a statistic.
— It is fashionable to object that those who have themselves
been victims of a collective guilt should not attempt to saddle
another people with such a burden; I wish to protest most
emphatically that this statement is based upon a misconception.
From Golgotha to Hitler, we have never been the victims of a
collective guilt, but of the lie of being collectively guilty.
— No one who lived in Germany during the Nazi persecution
of the Jews will be able to forget that tragedy so completely that
it will be as if it had never happened. It would be dishonest to
pretend that we can simply take up where we left off in 1933.
✡ *When I woke up, someone said:*
Many are drowned,
but you are saved.
But often the water still follows me. (Nelly Sachs)
— And the children inherit the fears of their parents.
— It all happened twenty years ago—is that a reason for forgetting it?
— We are the living reminders, the witnesses who were condemned and reprieved, and it is our duty not to allow our
neighbours to forget what happened.

— We are not concerned with hatred and revenge. But we cannot and we will not forget the past. We owe it to our dead to remember it.

✡ *Remembrance is the secret of redemption. (Baal Shem-Tov)*

— Nobody can forget the past and those who try to do so only succeed in distorting the memory of it. This generation has the duty to continue to bear witness, an inexorable duty not towards the dead but towards our children and future generations. But such a tragedy demands more of us than that we should be the accusers.

† *It is not fitting that we should expect the surviving Jews to forget, and certainly not that we should demand it of them. What opinion would we have of a people who forgot its own martyrs?*

† *. . . and in any case, the mass murder of the Jews has aroused so much revulsion that it will take more than one generation to cope with it.*

— In a way, it is always impossible for us to come to terms with the past, because what has happened cannot be influenced.

— The problem is not so much coming to terms with the past as coming to grips with the present and with the future.

— Nobody can undo the past . . . We can only see that the past has no future. The present is the only tense in which we can act.

— What matters is not that we should forget quickly, but that we should thoroughly forgive.

— Don't ask of us that we should forget, but you yourselves must remember so that we may one day forget.

— It is not necessary to forget anything; on the contrary, everything, even bad things, can be turned to account—they can serve as a warning so that instead of happening again they will eventually lead to positive consequences.

— Any Jew in Germany who today states his case, runs the risk of repeating what non-Jews have already said a thousand times. Once we were powerless, but now we can call the murderers of the past (like Eichmann) to account; the balance has been redressed. The memory of past sufferings remains, but it is no longer humiliating.

— The trials which, during the last few years, have recalled the

crimes of the past, were held not for our benefit but for the sake
of justice and future generations.

— It took a long time before the Germans themselves began to
investigate suspects: but now what really happened has at last
penetrated their German hide . . . that most of the Nazi criminals
being brought to trial these days have been discovered not by
surviving victims but by those who were not involved, by
Germans—former soldiers, policemen, civilians . . .

— The faces of the Germans have lost the last traces of their
defeat and of the hardships which followed; they look plump
and assured. Their nerves have recovered and they lead very
creditable lives. The whole world admires their efficiency . . . You
cannot become strong and successful without in the process
being guilty of making mistakes; that is true not only of Germans.
Together, we have been driven to the limit; what happened
between the Germans and the Jews was the extreme of human
behaviour. But they have survived safe and sound to take up
where they left off—they no longer remember the interval
between. They have come through unscathed—that is what
worries me, that is what makes me feel afraid of them . . .

Because of what has happened, our lives are irrevocably connected. Persecutor and persecuted remain involved with each
other. This has nothing to do with guilt or innocence. I certainly
don't wish to imply that the victim, simply because he is a victim,
is therefore innocent. But persecutor and persecuted will for
ever afterwards bear a stigma on their foreheads—the same
stigma of the persecution which binds them together. And so I
am involved with the Germans and they are involved with
me . . .

— We cannot and we must not forget what the Germans have
done to the Jewish people. But we must not respond with hatred
where there is a genuine awareness of guilt and a genuine desire
to atone. It is unworthy of a Jew to make hatred a motive for
action. It is our duty to contribute towards a better future whenever we have the opportunity—however small. I believe this
opportunity exists for us also in Germany. It is the essence of
Judaism to bring people together, which we can serve, it seems

to me, at any time and in any place. We should do so even in Germany—especially in Germany.

— All these investigations, recollections, reflections and realisations must be made to serve one overruling purpose: to bring about a good relationship between Jews and Germans—in spite of everything, or perhaps because of everything.

— The present-day philosemitism does not idealise the Jews, it does not patronise us and it is not a charitable gift—it has a therapeutic value for the Germans; it helps them to ease a little the burden of the past: it is a German cure for a German sickness. I don't think the Jews have the right to deny the Germans this self-help. For us it is neither good nor bad; it does not really concern us at all.

— The philosemitic reaction to the past is a kind of German self-defence: they withdraw from the atrocities which their people committed by sympathising with the victims—not because they are Jews, but because they were the victims.

† *The sinister guilt, which cannot be seen as concerning individuals, produces a sinister advantage, a sort of safe-conduct.*

✡ *As long as the Jews are kept behind a protective wall built of shyness, bad conscience and good intentions, no genuine relationship can develop—it merely turns them into 'untouchables'.*

† *Not only psychological and political considerations cause our Jewish citizens to feel uneasy. There used to live more than twenty thousand Jews here in Cologne, today there are about twelve hundred. They can hardly wish for life to go on as if nothing had happened. (Heinrich Böll)*

✡ *They live in a country where their presence (or more accurately, their imagined presence, since many young West Germans have never knowingly met a Jew) calls forth symptoms of profound and often irrational anxiety. Guilt has produced both the urge to make amends and a certain resentment. The struggle between these feelings makes many Jews uneasy. While they go about their daily lives as often as not unidentified as Jews, the Germans wrestle with ghosts.*

— A little while ago my eight-year-old daughter came to show me that she had inked a number on her arm. My wife almost fainted, but the little one said: 'I want to have my number just like Mummy and Daddy.'

† *Their sleep is still disturbed by dreams in which Hitler's hench-men are still at work exterminating six million people like them-selves—men, women, children, young and old, rich and poor; a firm step outside their house recalls the times when they lived in constant fear of the Gestapo; they are still startled when the door-bell rings: they have come for us! And so they live amongst us, with their memories which will always be with them: Jews who survived the camps or returned from exile to postwar Germany.*

— We are slowly recovering physically and emotionally. The knowledge that we are no longer second-class citizens gives us confidence. But we are still extremely vulnerable, and we are frequently upset by things which in themselves are quite unim-portant . . . For instance, if the door-bell rings persistently when we don't expect anyone it may terrify us for a moment, though afterwards we are amused at ourselves, because of course we no longer have to be afraid of the Gestapo.

— It often happens to me at night that I see them, the ghosts of Mordechai Tannenbaum from Warsaw, of Jechiel Scheinbaum from Vilna, of Fruma Plotnicka from Bendzin, and I can hear them saying to me: We perished—and you have survived. And I ask my conscience, what shall I say to Mordechai, Jechiel and Fruma?

— Probably most people who have survived the camps sooner or later torment themselves with the question why they should have been the ones to have survived . . .

— Whenever we commemorate the dead, our thoughts fre-quently turn to ourselves, who have survived accidently, and we question whether we have made the best possible use of the time granted to us and whether we are able to justify our survival. Year after year, this question arises, and it becomes more, not less, urgent.

We all of us have a bad conscience. It almost seems as if only those of our generation who died are quite without reproach, without fault or guilt. Their death was a true redemption, and we who have been left over without having deserved or earned

our survival will always be guilty. This is how it seems to us—
and is that why we are impatient, loud, nervous and dissatisfied?
— Whenever I shake hands with a German or am caught in a
crowded tram I start to tremble. I don't know whether I am
touching someone who took part . . .
— Perhaps I am only imagining it, but whenever I am amongst
people and somebody jostles me I wonder whether it was really
accidental. And then it occurs to me: For all I know, he may
have been there when they killed my father or my mother.
— Today, nobody could attack people because they are Jews
and get away with it. Antisemitism is unpopular in West
Germany. And so, from a practical point of view, life for the
Jews in Germany today runs much more smoothly than it did,
let us say, in the year 1930. Especially the authorities maintain an
attitude of almost patriarchal benevolence towards the few Jews
living in Germany today. But the authorities are not everything.
Daily, a Jew living in Germany comes into contact with the
average German. And here I must mention an uncanny feeling
—perhaps neurotic but not unjustified—the feeling experienced
by every, but every Jew who returns to Germany—a feeling
which slowly fades and disappears only after many years: who is
that man sitting next to me in the tram or in the cinema, standing
next to me in the queue or serving me from behind a counter?
Did he really push people into a gas chamber or did he perhaps
shout his hysterical approval when Hitler promised him the
final solution? How are we to know what his hands have done,
what his eyes have seen?
— That is what makes it so difficult to live in this country: we
don't know where people were during the war and what they
may have done.
— Do you think it is easier for a non-Jew than for a Jew to shake
hands with the former commandant of a concentration camp?
— The problem which must be faced by every individual Jew
who lives in Germany for any length of time can be reduced to a
simple formula: How far can I, may I, shall I, trust people?
Trust people—that is a question which everyone has to answer
for himself.

— How does it feel to live as a Jew in Germany today? The answer to this question may vary slightly according to personal, social, professional and financial circumstances, according to local conditions, according to individual reactions, character, experiences and sensibility . . . that in this time and in this place he feels, again and again, estranged and astonished, anxious or insecure, alarmed and suspicious; in short: he feels uncomfortable.

And the reason why we sometimes feel so uncomfortable is because it seems to us that there are a great many Germans who certainly took no part in the exterminations and to whom it would never occur to commit atrocities, but who on the other hand also show no real signs of wanting to make amends and who do nothing towards ensuring a better future. Well, the Jews in Germany today have unintentionally acquired a sort of invisible detector, which sometimes registers what we would otherwise not realise.

There are in this country hundreds of thousands of people, ranging from those in the highest positions to simple country folk, who were and remain innocent towards us Jews, and intellectually and emotionally there is not a crack in the relationship between us. We are aware of this and we appreciate it. Hundreds of thousands. But what about the millions?

— Many Jews cannot be sure that their neighbour will shake hands with them and if he does, that his hands are clean. These agonizing doubts have caused many people to keep within their own small circle of friends. And if just those who were most concerned for their well-being objected to the erection of new ghetto walls, they ought to realise that we have been hurt, we are vulnerable, and we are afraid of being hurt again.

— It is perhaps natural that there is today a certain embarrassment between Jews and Germans. Indeed, it is no exaggeration to say that those Jews whose relationship with Germany was once especially close are the ones who are now most reserved and embarrassed.

— . . . something almost pathological in the relationship between the Jews and the Germans. The bad conscience of the Germans has resulted in a special uncritical friendliness, which is

6*

often not quite sincere; and the Jews feel resentful and therefore uneasy and even guilty about living in this country. Both attitudes are unhealthy and make it impossible for people to feel relaxed and satisfied with each other.

— Whatever happens, whenever I sit together with non-Jews, the shadow of the past seems to darken everything. When they talk of their wartime experiences, and there is nothing sinister about that—don't people in other countries do the same?—it brings to my mind the image of the uniform worn by those who killed my brother. When they discuss a current problem in Germany, I begin to wonder whether there are echoes of yesterday in what they are saying . . .

— Perhaps you think that I am much too sensitive. You may be right. But I have reason to be sensitive. To be exact: I have six million reasons. I would like people to assess me at last according to who I am, according to my good and bad qualities, and not according to Nazi prejudices. I would like to be able to meet people without embarrassing them . . .

— Even young Germans cannot meet us without betraying a sort of conditioned response. Their eyes begin to shine and they become quite excited: Ah, you are a Jew, how interesting! You are the first Jew I have met. Of course I know all about what happened in the past, and I know what people say about the Jews today. But I would very much like to form my own opinion . . . And then come the endless questions, the analysis. Everywhere, every day, Jews in Germany encounter this sort of response. We would prefer it if people could accept us as we are, as we have become through our experiences: as fellow human beings, fellow citizens, as people who have shared the fate of our time. We would prefer not to be singled out—for good or evil— as relics of old prejudices, we would like to be treated at last like everybody else.

— Our greatest worry is not the present but the leap from the past into the future. And if we want to be quite honest we have to admit that not only are the Germans unable to meet us without making us feel that we are embarrassing them, but we ourselves are unable to behave naturally towards our non-Jewish neigh-

bours. We would like to forget what happened during the time of
the Nazis—on the condition that the Germans will not forget it.
— One has to look back in order to find one's appointed place
in the present.
— From a social, political and religious point of view the Jews
in Germany today are safer—in spite of the residual antisemitism
—than at any other time in German history; yet the relationship
between Jews and non-Jews here is a burning question. It is
much more than the problem of a minority. The circumstances
of the Jews in Germany and the attitude of the Germans towards
them have achieved a symbolical significance.
— There is no generally valid answer to the question: is a
dialogue between Jews and Germans possible? It is just as difficult
to argue with a nationalistic Jew as with German nationalists.
People should stop generalising about the Jews and the Germans.
— I have said that the relationship between Jews and Germans
is an insoluble problem. I did not mean that it is hopeless.
— Admittedly, prejudice, hatred and antisemitism continue to
exist in Germany, and sometimes the evidence of this is almost
frightening. Anyone who is not hopelessly naive or wilfully blind
will have to agree with this. On the other hand, it is certainly
equally true that many honest attempts are now being made by
the Germans to come to terms with the past. The associations for
Christian-Jewish collaboration and other movements, conferences
and exhibitions all bear witness that the Jews, who not all that
long ago were outlawed and persecuted, now arouse a quite
different interest in the German people.
— No other people has ever shown itself so receptive to
Jewish thought as the Germans do now; one might almost say
that they long for Jewish values. Confronted with this evolution,
and surrounded by a resurgent antisemitism, the Jews in Germany
have work to do which gives them the chance of having a future
there.
— The Jewish people, the Jewish religion and the meaning of
Judaism have become of topical interest to thousands upon
thousands. In groups of 100, 200, 300 they come, especially young
people, workers, soldiers, schoolchildren, students, etc., to see the

synagogue, to attend divine services and to visit the community centre.

— We have faith in the young people, they come to us, and they want to learn, they are very anxious to learn.

— I don't know whether to call it open-mindedness or curiosity. But it is a fact that we have non-Jewish visitors almost every day. I try to explain to them our customs and our rites. It is very gratifying to be able to show our synagogue to about 500 young people and to talk to them afterwards about Judaism. They ask questions like: what is Judaism, who is a Jew, what is your divine service like, what prayers do you say, to whom do you pray? They always look most surprised when I explain to them that there are some prayers which Jews and Christians have in common, the Psalms for instance, or when I tell them that Jesus, Paul and Peter, etc., were Jews. Nobody leaves the synagogue; the young people are prepared to listen for hours. Therefore, I have to admit it: something new is happening. Non-Jews are coming to the synagogues in really large numbers for information—that is something which has never happened before. Here it is becoming commonplace. Such encounters don't leave people unaffected.

XV

JEWS IN GERMANY TODAY

— The Jewish remnant in Germany—a short postscript.

— . . . that their Jewishness is a burden and they will never again be light of heart.

— Thirty thousand individual experiences.

— . . . that the Jews in Germany today think of their lives there as a short postscript to the history of German Jewry.

— It is too early to say whether the postscript may perhaps at some future point be seen as a prelude.

— Not we but life has decided that there should be a Jewish community in Germany today.

— The survivors are few in number; they are important only because they have inherited the consequences of the holocaust.

— 'Twenty years' means to most people a passage of time. But to the survivors of the concentration camps it means the period of their regeneration.

✡ *The Jews in Germany today can be seen and understood only against the background of modern Germany. This much-analysed, much misunderstood country, in fact, can be understood better once the current chapter in the history of its Jews is closely examined. The Jewish story itself is part of the German story.*

— Things are not easy for the Jews who are living in Germany today. Their religious life cannot flourish while there are so few of them. And while there are so few of them, they will not be recognised by the Germans as a political force. But as a moral force the Jews in Germany today have to be reckoned with. This does not depend on the size of their community but on the fact that such a community exists.

— Before 1933 there were 500,000 Jews living in Germany; of these, almost none are left. The 30,000 Jews who are living in Germany today come from Russia, Poland, Hungary . . .

— The number of the Jews whose families have lived in

Germany for generations is small and grows steadily smaller.

— One has to realise that what we call the remnant of European Jewry is a collection of groups of the most varied origins. They come from different countries and different strata of society, they speak different languages, and cutting across these differences there are also the differences of their cultural and political backgrounds and of their individual characteristics.

— Actually, we are all of us refugees, people without roots; some of us have settled at random after being driven from our homes abroad, others were exiled and have returned.

— We are not the continuation of the former community; unlike it we are not a homogeneous and well-defined group; we are the result of chance or an historical imperative. We are the remnant, we are the rescued; we come from all sorts of places and have been influenced by all sorts of circumstances, experiences, and systems of education.

— . . . all of us shipwrecked and brought together by chance, to create out of the confusion a sort of community.

— Today the Jewish community in West Germany consists of 26,000 Jews, scattered over 500 places and forming 70 communities. It is assumed that there are a further 10,000 who are Jews but not registered with the communities, and possibly another 10,000 who no longer consider themselves to be Jews.

— Almost none of the communities have maintained the old tradition of having their own rabbi, cantor, or teacher of Hebrew and religious knowledge.

— Only six of the communities have more than a thousand members. Most of the large towns have no more than a few hundred Jews.

— The members of the various communities often live far apart, so that the community may be spread across a district of more than 100 miles.

— . . . so that a large number of communities cannot be defined geographically; their members often live scattered over a vast area. At least 2,000 Jews are today living dispersed over a few hundred places none of which have their own community—a sort of diaspora within the diaspora.

— It is generally predicted that Jewish life in Germany will in future centre upon a dozen or so of the larger towns.

— Although the present communities are constitutionally a sort of continuation of the old type of religious congregation, they certainly cannot be compared with the old Jewish communities which were the culmination of centuries of development. The dynamics of the new communities are quite different. One might almost say that they arose out of the modern impulse of people who have in some way been deprived to form associations to safeguard their common interests. But as the effects of the persecution amounted to so much more than mere deprivation, the members are held together by 'the shared Jewish experience' . . .

— Even the large communities in West Germany today are still smaller than the medium-sized communities in the second decade of this century. And there are also very small communities, with so few members that they recall the earliest Jewish settlements of the Middle Ages. In the larger communities—and all those who have more than 200 members have to be included in this category—Jewish life has gradually developed since 1945. Community and youth centres have been built, for the children there are courses in Hebrew and religious knowledge, on the High Holy Days the various groups may each hold their own divine services, and more and more cultural events and lectures of general interest are being arranged. But things are very different in the smaller communities, and for people who live beyond easy reach of the nearest Jewish centre. . . . that Jews complain about their terrible loneliness. They feel cut off from Jewish life and would so much like to be in touch. When it comes to arranging events, neither the contents nor the standard of the programme are of primary importance. People value any occasion which brings them together, out of the naive desire not to be alone.

— The extent of social relations with non-Jews depends upon the composition and the size of the community: it is directly related to the proportion of community members who were born in Germany and inversely to the proportion of former DP's; but it also depends upon the number of Jews living locally; the

fewer Jews there are, the more involved they are in social relations with non-Jews. Of all the Jews living in Germany today,
the former DP's from Eastern Europe are least inclined to have
social relations with non-Jews . . . in many East European
families a tradition engendered by the memory of childhood experiences, by habit and by emotional inclination, fights a stub-
born rearguard action against German influences.

— There are East European and West European Jews, Jews
who practise their religion and Jews who don't, survivors, exiles
who have returned and newcomers; the communities are bound
to fail in their efforts to provide a suitable social environment—
which is a tragedy for the many Jews without relations who need
some outside interest and a feeling of belonging, and it is
especially a tragedy for the old. There is a grave danger that the
Jewish communities in Germany will fail to become sanctuaries
for all those people who are too old to live in exile or to emigrate,
which was the final justification for their existence, which even
their Jewish critics abroad had to concede.

— We are living today in post-Jewish circumstances, by which
I mean that our actual everyday existence does not grant us any
direct Jewish experiences.

— The fewer Jews there are in a place and the fewer Jewish
activities there are, the more Jews are attracted to the synagogue
—in the smaller communities, the proportion of Jews attending
the Sabbath services is three times as great as in the larger ones.
In 53 communities the membership falls below 100, which makes
the observance of religious tradition difficult if not actually impossible, because according to religious laws, it usually requires
the presence of at least ten adult male Jews. In fact, twenty of
these smaller communities have no more than ten to fifteen adult
male members.

— Religion has ceased to be a matter of individual opinion and
become instead a means of expressing one's membership of the
Jewish community. For the sake of belonging to the Jewish
community we pretend to others and to ourselves that we are
expressing an inner religious impulse. But let no one make the
mistake of regarding this as an admission of a conscious dis-

honesty; many of the Jews in Germany try sincerely to find ways of manifesting their Jewishness. They are like the Marranos, they are not used to expressing their Jewishness and do it so to speak experimentally.

Even if some of the leaders and many of the members do not live as Jews, nevertheless they live very much for the Jewish community. All the activities of the congregation take place for the sake of the congregation, and the congregation becomes once more the Jewish community—or at least the only thing that exists in its place. It has been termed, a little maliciously, an association of Jewish sympathisers, an association for the encouragement of certain peculiarities called 'Jewish tradition'— which is observed out of reverence (or a feeling of guilt?) and for which the individual has a sort of benevolent affection.

— There are almost no rabbis, Jewish scholars or people who have their roots in Jewish culture and religion; those there are enjoy no special esteem and are called upon only for advice, and that only occasionally.

— The Jewish community in Germany is extremely short of intellectuals and has almost no full time religious officials. Teachers of Hebrew and religious knowledge, cantors, youth leaders, social workers, Jewish butchers and beadles, and in East European communities even the rabbis, all have other occupations with which they earn their living. Community affairs are managed by honorary officials.

— The intellectual level of the Jews in Germany today is below the average, compared with that of non-Jews as well as with that of Jewish communities elsewhere. The reason for this is the completely different social structure.

— There is no Jewish leadership capable of rousing the masses from their lethargy and of influencing their way of thinking. We simply do not have enough people who are able and willing to serve the Jewish community.

— There are not enough librarians, lecturers, historians, lawyers and doctors, amongst the Jews living in Germany today, and there are also not enough social workers and people of every kind suited to initiate, organise and run public institutions.

Because the Jewish communities do not have these people, they also do not have an adequate cultural and social life.

— It has to be admitted that the present community is a mere shadow of the former German Jewish community, not only because it is so small, but also because it is so unimportant. Not even the very high positions reached by some of its members can disguise this fact.

— Population: The average age is alarmingly high: almost 50. Only 15 per cent are below the age of 20. From this (and from the poor physical and mental health which is the result of the persecution) there follow crucial consequences. Of the roughly 30,000 Jews, no more than 8,000 earn their own living, because almost 30 per cent (8,000 to 10,000) are more than 60 years old and are mostly retired and live on their pensions, reparation payments or public assistance. Of the 8,000 Jews who are gainfully occupied only about half have succeeded in re-establishing themselves successfully. About 2,000 of them have their own business. There are very few independent professionals (about 250 lawyers and no more than a few dozens in other professions); there are even fewer civil servants and other employees. There are perhaps about 150 Jewish students in German universities and colleges. A political economist would say that the Jews in Germany today are very definitely middle class; the extremes—great wealth and dire poverty—are almost non-existent.

— At the beginning of this decade, the percentage of Jews receiving pensions was double that of the German population, and the 1,200 Jews totally dependent upon relief was a larger element in German Jewry than the few rich members. The majority of the old pensioners, like the majority of business and professional people, had middle-class incomes and lived according to middle-class standards.

— It is no secret that most of the nightclubs run for the benefit of American soldiers in Germany are owned or managed by Jews. This is one of the causes of open hostility between the East European and the native German Jews, to whom it is a constant cause of annoyance that the majority of nightclubs are run by Jews from Eastern Europe.

— The term 'self-employed' ought not to be accepted at face-value. Jews are naturally enterprising and prefer to be their own masters, but under the circumstances the term implies a sort of social verdict. As far as the DP's are concerned, their lack of command of the German language precludes most of them from being employed, and amongst the exiles who have returned, age as well as the desire to 'arrive' plays a part. This urge to be independent is in reality nothing more than an admission of a lack of training or skill and expresses in economic terms the isolation of Germany's 'new Jews'.

— Eventually, the leaders of the various Jewish communities realised that the religious observances, the existence of the community and their shared Jewishness by themselves were not enough to make their members feel sufficiently committed to a common cause, and as a final remedy they added the force and meaning of Zionism to provide the necessary rallying-point for their efforts.

Circulars sent out by the communities on festive occasions invite the members to donate money for Israel instead of asking for contributions to the community funds. The education provided by the communities for their children and young people has a Zionist slant, even when emigration to Israel is not its aim. Sermons, addresses, lectures, inaugural or opening speeches all put such a very special emphasis on the existence of Israel, that many observers cannot resist the temptation of regarding the existing German-Jewish communities as collecting centres and nurseries for Israel.

✡ *The survivors have drawn the consequences . . . Young people emigrate to Israel; the others give their moral and material support to the efforts made in the diaspora on behalf of Israel.*

— Money for the Jewish National Fund: a sort of indulgence bought for the sin of living here and not there.

— Immediately after the war they were in need of help—but now they are helping . . .

✡ *The reality of the Jewish State, where many of them have near relatives, has strengthened the self-assurance of the German Jews.*

— There is nothing unnatural about having two loyalties; some of the comets and all the planets run their courses with two focal points.

— We identify not with past history but with a living Judaism, which does not exist exclusively in the actual land of Israel but may be a vital and effective element anywhere in the world.

— Our commitment to Israel is not political, but spiritual and emotional.

— And so we endeavour to establish an active community here in Germany, even though we shall continue to regard Israel as our spiritual home.

— We are no longer second-class citizens, which means that we have not only the same rights as other people, but also the same obligations. The State has dealt fairly with us (and let nobody start objecting, because not everyone has received all his reparation payments, or because here and there a formerly prominent Nazi is once again in a position of power; these are minor details and do not belong to the general outline which I am attempting to draw). The State, then, has dealt fairly with us; our duty: to be loyal to the State. There are occasions when our community fails to act in this spirit. For instance, we display in our assembly rooms a picture of Herzl, and on special occasions we hang next to it the Israeli flag; this is perfectly all right and could not be otherwise, because Herzl has done great things for us and we love Israel with all our heart. But—we are citizens of West Germany, this is where we live, and we are treated as equals by the Germans. In view of this, ought we not to display on festive occasions the black, red and gold flag next to the blue and white one?

— We consider it of importance to arouse in our young people not only a love for Israel and the Jewish religion, but also to teach them a thorough knowledge of their environment. If our children are not to grow up in mental ghettoes, it is essential that we should encourage in them a positive attitude towards Germany

— This is the environment in which our children are living; we want to give them at least the chance of feeling at home in it.

Their education has to fulfil the needs of the diaspora; that is the first requirement, whether we like it or not.

— Our children and young people attend German schools; they are in a precarious position, demanding from them a special degree of intellectual independence. We have to make the choice. Either we bring them up in the spirit and for the purpose of life in Israel, or their education will have to be adjusted to the civilization in which they happen to live, without of course suppressing their impulse to belong to the Jewish people.

— They attend German schools, become apprenticed and begin to work in German concerns, they make friends with young Germans and share the general German preoccupations. Outwardly—at school, at work, in conversation with their non-Jewish contemporaries—there is almost nothing which distinguishes them, they seem to have adopted the same ideas and ideals. But at home they are suddenly no longer so sure: here Germany and the Germans continue to mean what they meant before 1945 ... At home, children and young people realise that their future lies in Israel, America, or some other country, but not in Germany.

— They are very assimilated and at the same time know that they do not belong: that sums up the position of most of the Jewish children in Germany today. In addition, they are aware that their existence there is only temporary. This temporary arrangement may under certain circumstances last for years or —the whole of their childhood.

— As they grow older they become more realistic: they have to finish their studies, they have to learn a profession or trade, before they will be able seriously to consider their emigration. Meanwhile, they are living 'for the time being' in Germany. It is precisely the peculiar effect of this experience of living in Germany 'for the time being'—which may in fact mean for decades—which makes the rising Jewish generation in Germany different from their Jewish contemporaries in other countries.

— Israel provides a clear orientation for some of the young people caught between the instability of adolescence and the insecurity of their actual lives; but they are then forced to make a distinction between themselves and their Jewish and non-Jewish contemporaries—they come to look down upon the others in some way. It is the means by which they themselves become a small but self-reliant group.

— The decision to emigrate to Israel often costs them years of amicable but obstinate struggle with their parents. 'Wouldn't you expect them to try to keep their children with them in Germany?' The parents have got used to living there, they are enjoying the economic miracle, and their children can go to school in peace and afterwards they can study. And then? Well, then all the world is open to them . . .

— Our parents don't want us to join the Zionist Youth Movement in Germany. But on the other hand, they want us to mix with other Jewish people of our own age. This inconsistency unintentionally causes their children a great deal of unhappiness. A boy of, say, twelve years of age, can feel that the time has come for him to reach a decision. But his parents would prefer him to remain undecided and don't seem to understand that this is impossible.

— Where the Jewish youth centres and the local groups of the Zionist Youth Movement do not co-operate they are in fierce competition—with ideological undertones—with each other: the members of the youth centres accuse the young Zionists that their movement encourages them to despise the communities and to reject the Jews of the diaspora, and they cite the example of young Zionists who are ashamed of being Jews, that is, who after ceasing to be members of the Youth Movement avoid all contact with the Jewish community. It is almost as if Zionists who leave the Youth Movement and do not emigrate to Israel saw no alternative except assimilation. In fact the Zionist Youth Movement refuses to admit that it is possible to live as a Jew in Germany today.

— A few places have other Jewish youth organisations besides the youth centres and the Zionist Youth Movement; they were established partly to provide additional activities, partly as necessary alternatives, and partly to give Jewish and non-Jewish young people an opportunity to work together. Israelis are the leading spirits not only in the Zionist Youth Movement but also in the youth centres, and Israel is the central theme around which all their activities revolve. The main difference is, that the Zionist Youth Movement prepares its members for emigration to Israel, and that the youth centres, while approving of emigration, do not consider it imperative.

Jewish education in Germany today no longer centres upon religious observances. The teaching of Hebrew and Jewish history, the activities of the youth organisations and the holiday centres, are all intended to propagate a knowledge of Israel and loyalty to the Jewish State.

— Many of those who returned from Israel brought with them children who were born in that country and who are now growing up in Germany. To these young people, being Israelis means more than their nationality. It means that they belong there and not here, and the majority of them intend to return to Israel after they have finished their studies. Young people who were born in Germany after the war are in a different position. To them Germany is their home; German is their language and they have never been to Israel. To save these children from mental and emotional solitude and from assimilation ... For being a Jew amongst non-Jews means to be the odd one out, because of the small number of Jews in Germany it may perhaps mean being the only Jewish pupil or apprentice, it may perhaps mean being met with a certain reserve amongst ones equals, difficulty in finding a marriage partner, etc.

— The question of mixed marriages is of the greatest importance for our future, because at the moment there are only two possibilities for us in Germany. Because there are so few young Jews living here today, mixed marriages happen quite often. Even someone who is not an observant Jew recognises a certain obligation towards his religion and the old traditions of Judaism. Will we bring up our children to be Jews or will we be saying: throughout my childhood I had to justify my existence and I will make things easier for my children—they shall grow up as Christians, so that they will not have to face similar problems later on. (Or the other side of the coin: to emigrate to Israel.

Because in America, England or France one is also likely to meet antisemitism.) We are all of us afraid of a repetition of what happened, but here the government and a large part of the press fight against antisemitism and one may hope that it can never happen again in Germany.

— One can hardly expect the community leaders to provide an educational programme which will encourage the young to emigrate, or not to provide them with a Jewish education at all —both extremes would endanger the future of the communities of which they are the founders and which they are serving daily with such energy and devotion. There seems to be no alternative to the solution indicated by an analysis of the personal problems with which they are confronted: They must no longer suppress the feeling of guilt from which they have suffered for about twenty years because they did not emigrate or because they returned; they must discuss the problem openly and allow their children to draw their own conclusions and to act accordingly. Whatever way the decision would fall, it would at least be a decision and they would no longer be evading the issue. It would be the best thing that could happen not only for the children but also for their parents, for whose 'guilt' the children would have the chance to 'atone'.

— The few young Jewish people living in Germany today have unequivocally decided that their future lies in Israel—seen historically, this is a sad postscript to the tragedy of German Jewry.

— Generally speaking, the feeling of the young people for Israel is strengthened by their lack of feeling for Germany.

— Only a small proportion of the young people will remain in Germany. It is a question of their future.

— What is at stake is the future of the whole Jewish community in Germany.

— The next generation will decide the future of the Jews in Germany.

† *How poor Germany has become without the Jews . . .*
† *We suffer from the guilt which we have inherited from the*

Nazis; we also suffer because of them from a national deficiency of Jews. Doubtlessly it would be better for the spiritual health of our country if we were still blessed with Jewish talent, with the affectionate criticism, the wit, the sharp reasoning of the Jews. Our literature, our music, and above all our press would be better, and perhaps we ourselves would have a better understanding of Germany.

† *Actually we do not have a Jewish problem in Germany. There is of course the German problem . . .* .

† *The opinion which we can expect other people to have of us will depend upon the opinion which we have of our Jews.*

† *The constitution of the Federal Republic clearly determines the official attitude towards its Jewish citizens. Paragraph 3 declares that all citizens shall be equal before the law regardless of their sex, origin, race, language, country of birth, faith, or religious or political opinions.*

✡ *An extreme demonstration of anxiety is the building of magnificent synagogues for minute congregations . . . The behaviour of the Germans is even more influenced by the past than that of the Jews.*

— New synagogues are being built out of public funds, the authorities look after the old Jewish cemeteries, and above all there are the reparation payments, for which one sometimes has to wait an inordinately long time—but they do get paid and they have helped many.

— There are in Hamburg today 1,380 Jews amongst a population of 1·8 million inhabitants. Yet a huge Jewish hospital is being built there. There will be neither enough Jewish doctors nor enough Jewish nurses for it, and certainly not enough Jewish patients. So why is this hospital being built?

It must be obvious to everybody that the large new Jewish hospital in Hamburg is intended as a gesture: that the municipality and the inhabitants of the town have contributed generously as a sort of demonstration—against the tormentors and for the tormented.

† *If you want to know why we have taken the time and the trouble to rebuild the old synagogue in Worms, and why it has given us so much satisfaction to do so, I will tell you: mainly for the sake of the brotherhood of men and because there have been Jews living in Worms*

for many centuries. The municipality has decided to look after the synagogue until we will once again have a Jewish community here.

† *'Jews and Germans'—as if the Jews who are living amongst us were not Germans, as if they were not just as much at home here as we ourselves. One may talk of Jews, Catholics, Protestants and Dissenters, but together they constitute the German people, within which all of them enjoy the same rights, are protected by the same laws, and must above all be considered equals.*

† *If we really want to atone and to make amends the best thing we can do is to re-educate our people to regard the Jews not as different, as foreign, but as human beings like ourselves, as our brothers.*

✡ *The primary goal of moral reparation was eradicating the traces of the pogrom of the mind, the Jewish character assassination by Nazi teachings.*

— How many people of good will are there in Germany? One cannot measure a positive power quantitatively. In importance they may well outweigh the larger number of those who do not care.

— We have to choose between trusting and not trusting them. That is a risk which we always have to take; from this decision every other will follow.

— *'Every Jew who survived survived in spite of us.'* I am alive in spite of them, I tell myself, in spite of them and yet among them. What does this 'in spite of' amount to? Has it made me intransigent and obstinate, this defiance, has it made me hate the people who would have killed me if I had not fled to another country and found another home, in spite of them?

— I once dreamed that the Nazis had set fire to the hut in which I was living. I had the opportunity of saving one single book from the flames. I stood before the burning hut and asked myself which meant more to me, the Bible or Faust. I could not make up my mind. And so in my dream they were both burned, the Bible and Faust.

— There may be Jews in Chicago, the Congo, in Siberia or in Frankfurt-on-the-Main who dream at night that they have been recognised as Jews at some German street corner, and wake up with a shock. That is a nightmare. Less than thirty years ago the synagogues were burned in Germany and the Jews were gassed. Today, Jews may well feel safer in Berlin or Nuremberg than in Capetown or Moscow.

— It simply isn't possible to continue in Germany now the natural process which was so brutally and senselessly destroyed. True, the synagogues have been restored to us. But it will be more difficult to restore our confidence.

— Certainly, they have built us some beautiful synagogues and they are paying us reparations; but intellectually and morally almost nothing has been done. Within the near future the Jewish communities will have neither rabbis nor teachers. There is not a single properly appointed Jewish school in the whole of West Germany.

— In the thirties Germany was cleared of its Jews—has it been cleared of its antisemites within the last twenty years? How can anyone be sure that the Germans (although they have become more sensitive to foreign opinion) will not one day burn the new synagogues, too? What has become of all the German Jew-haters and their equipment of pseudo-scholarship? Should one not save the Germans (let us not consider the Jews) from re-newed danger—and prevent rather than further a new symbiosis? Would it not be more considerate to avoid doing anything which might lead to renewed suffering for the Germans and for the Jews? The rest of the world is no paradise. But—there has been only one Auschwitz in the twentieth century.

— The secret soul of the individual Jew in Germany today or, as we once used to say, German Jew, is of no significance to the course of history. What went on and what goes on there will before long die with him and be also forgotten. In public affairs they are of no consequence. They present no obstacle to the steam-roller of history. But in the final analysis, perhaps the individual matters more than history, which anyway makes no sense to the individual.

— And I have to admit that I find life difficult—especially psychologically. I am worried about the future, because I wonder whether we will ever cease to be second-class citizens. There are indications to the contrary. I do not believe in the resurgence of organised antisemitism. Nevertheless, we are worried. We would like to be treated as equals and not merely tolerated. Tolerance seems to me a terrible word—it is a substitute for rights and justice.

— I think that a Jew who regards himself as a citizen of the world, given courage and strength, can return to Germany to co-operate with the positive forces here, and to renew the fruitful symbiosis which simply has to be kept alive. I would like to make my own small contribution towards turning Germany into a democracy. But I cannot do this if I find myself always in a special position; I have to be made to feel that I belong.

— Today, we are again first class citizens in Germany, living in a democracy; as citizens we enjoy our rights and fulfil our obligations. We feel that we owe it to the State to be loyal to it, and we are. But no one who is liberal-minded, no decent German, will expect us at this stage to feel again entirely at home.

— Jews and Germans have to be able to live together. One would think that after the extreme events of the past, Jews and Germans would find the way to each other in an extraordinary, historically unique manner. Compared with their relationship to other peoples, they are in a special position towards each other.

✡ *So let us be Germans and Jews. Let us be both, without worrying about the 'and', indeed, without even mentioning it—but really both. How—that is basically a matter of tact. (Franz Rosenzweig)*

— They were exiled and they returned, even this time. Perhaps this time this sad Odyssey will finally have reached its happy ending? Perhaps now they are definitely reconciled? Jews are again living in Germany. They are Germans and still merely Jews; they are Jews and nevertheless they are Germans. Certainly, we must not forget the past; it shall remain alive in our hearts as a warning: it shall continue to remind us that we are human beings, that we are simply human beings.

— Is it possible to live in a country for any length of time, and even to raise children there, if one has a bad conscience about it? If one doesn't dare to admit abroad where one lives permanently? ... that divided attitude of people who on the one hand say no to Jewish life in Germany, but on the other have been living here for a good many years and hold important office within the Jewish community. Surely they no longer expect to be taken seriously when they continue to insist at every opportunity that they don't really live here permanently. Such protestations are a gesture which they feel they owe to their conscience.

— Every few years they go abroad, in order to maintain their right of entry into some other country, or their right of residence in it. But almost all of them come back again, because the older they get and the more they get used to living in Germany, the harder it becomes for them to begin again somewhere else.

— People who have been living in Germany for years or even decades can no longer expect to give the impression that they are ready to leave at a moment's notice. The Jewish community in Germany must have the courage of its existence.

— I know quite a few families who have emigration visas to the U.S.A. and who go there every few years for a few months in order to keep the visas valid—having one foot there and the other in Germany.

— I know, it sounds crazy, but every time when I hear that another important Nazi has been arrested we begin to make plans to leave. Is it possible not to feel insecure here in Germany?

— We are still ready to leave at a moment's notice. We used to have a few German friends, really nice people, who by now have lost all interest in us because we were really always intending to leave. And we have some Jewish friends, with whom we sit every Friday evening and discuss our emigration.

— There are many small vexations which are hardly noticeable and don't upset anybody, but which are slowly making our life here in Germany unbearable. And so it is still always possible that the Jews will gradually leave, that a general indifference will lead to the result which Hitler failed to achieve in spite of all his plans for exterminating the Jews: the final solution of the Jewish problem in Germany.

✡ *Several thousand exiles who have returned betray their ambivalence by keeping their foreign nationality. Israelis and citizens of other nations which permit them to do this often re-acquired their German citizenship.*

✡ *Some German Jews remain citizens of their new countries and do not return permanently, but live and work in Germany for more or less unlimited periods. Particularly influential are half-returned guest lecturers and professors. A number of Jewish businessmen also spend much, most, or all of their time in their former homeland. Unable to decide on returning permanently, they come back as intercontinental commuters and give many people the impression of being permanent residents.*

— The question frequently arises whether or not it is possible for Jews to live in Germany today. If the Jews would have to leave Germany, you could work out on the fingers of one hand for how long democrats and Christians and all sorts of nonconformists and other people who believe in freedom of conscience and choice could and would still want to live there. And what would happen to Germany's relationship with the rest of the world?

— If the Jews will one day again have to leave Germany, it will signal the end of German democracy.

Perhaps time will bring about the final solution of the Jewish problem in Germany, in spite of the fact that there are many decent Germans and many Jews who have a blind faith in the country, and in spite of the fact that the world is now standing guard. The statistics of the Jewish population show unequivocally that the various new Jewish community centres which have just been established will not be in use for long, because the older generation will die out and the next generation lives with the intention of emigrating to Israel or some other country. I think I am right in saying that during the past year only one Jewish child has been born to this large community. It is not difficult to work out the size of the Jewish population twenty years from now. I don't think many more of the exiles will return. I can't imagine that Jews abroad, who may have cherished the thought of one day returning to Germany, would still dare to do so now.

— Few children are born to the Jews in Germany; emigration continues and natural causes make for an ever-increasing death-rate; the Jewish population will get smaller and smaller. Probably a steady trickle of elderly and old people will continue to return; the future of the Jews in Germany and the kind of Jewish life to be found there will literally be determined by old age.

✡ *The community as a whole seems to lack the will to survive; mixed marriages are frequent and most of the children of these unions are lost to Judaism. Perhaps these last Jews in Germany feel that the time has come to let their community die and are willing to let it happen.*

✡ *From a purely biological point of view, the Jewish community in Germany is dying out.*

— We will come to the end of our time and there will be nobody to succeed us.

— Our community consists mainly of old people, who will soon leave us for ever. The rising generation will either assimilate or emigrate. And the rest will be condemned to bury the rest.